Recipes From Iowa With Love

By

PEG HEIN

and

KATHRYN CRAMER

Illustrated by
Kathryn Cramer

W9-CPV-696

From Tom + Karen Graves (Daniel + Kelly, too) from wedding July 1986

Copyright © 1982 by Peg Hein and Kathryn Cramer

All rights reserved.

No part of this book may be reproduced in any form or by any means without permission in writing from the publisher.

Edited by Dorothy Yeglin

Design and Typesetting by
Type Design House, Inc.
522 Eleventh Street
Des Moines, Iowa

Published by New Boundary Designs, Inc.
1453 Park Rd.
Chanhassen, MN 55317

Ordering information for additional copies is located at the back of the book.

Cover Design: *"From Iowa... With Love"*
Copyright © 1981 by Young Creations, Inc. Exclusive distribution rights held by New Boundary Designs, Inc.

ISBN: 0-913703-01-X

First Printing, 1982
Second Printing, 1983
Third Printing, 1985

In "Recipes From Iowa... With Love" we have collected favorite recipes from fine cooks throughout Iowa and combined them with highlights of history, places and people that make our state unique. Most of the recipes are easy to prepare for family meals and relaxed entertaining. Others are perfect for those special occasions when an unusual and memorable dish is called for. In looking at these recipes, we find that the cooking of Iowa, like its people, is varied, unpretentious and at times, elegant. We hope you enjoy using this book as much as we enjoyed creating it. Now, we give to you these

Recipes From Iowa... With Love,

Peggy Hein & Kathy Cramer

CONTENTS

Appetizers

Recipes from Iowa with Love...

The abundant supply of clam shells in the Mississippi River near Muscatine made this area the button-making capital of the world. In 1914, Muscatine had 35 button factories in operation. In recent years, plastic has replaced mother of pearl, and the industry has nearly vanished.

Muscatine Clam Dip

2 3-ounce packages cream cheese
¾ cup mayonnaise
1 small clove of garlic, crushed
1 7-ounce can minced clams, drained
¼ teaspoon salt
¼ teaspoon fresh ground pepper
½ teaspoon paprika
1 teaspoon Worcestershire sauce

Mix the cream cheese, mayonnaise and garlic together until smooth. Add minced clams and blend in with seasonings. Chill. Serve with crackers or raw vegetables.

Dill Toasts
"crunchy and seasoned just right for appetizers or snacks"

½ cup butter, softened
1 clove garlic, minced
½ teaspoon onion salt
¼ teaspoon celery seed
20 slices very thin
white bread
Dill weed
Salad seasoning

Mix butter, garlic, onion salt and celery seed together and spread on bread. Sprinkle dill weed and salad seasoning over the top to taste. Cut slices in half. Toast in 225° oven for 1½-2 hours or until very crisp and lightly browned. These are also good with soups and salads.

Iowans cultivate over 90 percent of their land, the largest percentage of any state in the nation. In fact, Iowa has one-fourth of the rich black soil that is rated premium in the United States. It's no wonder that the Hawkeye State is often called America's "bread basket."

Bread Basket Spread

"your guests will devour this"

Serves 14

1 cup sour cream
1 cup mayonnaise
1 package vegetable soup mix, Swiss style
2 tablespoons onion, chopped fine
1 10-ounce package frozen chopped spinach, thawed and drained
1 5-ounce can water chestnuts, grated
1 loaf unsliced crusty rye or pumpernickel bread

Combine all of the ingredients except bread. Cut 1" off the top of loaf of bread. Hollow out middle portion leaving ½" to form the shell for the dip. Cut removed bread into cubes. Serve with a small knife for spreading.

Great Mexican Aperitivos

Serves 12

2 pounds ground beef
1 cup chopped onion
1 package taco mix
2 cans bean dip
2 cups shredded Cheddar
   cheese
1 cup shredded Mozzarella
   cheese

Cook the meat, onion and taco mix in skillet till meat is lightly browned and onion tender. Drain. Lightly oil a 7×11½″ baking dish. Layer the bean dip and ground beef mixture. Mix the cheeses and spread over the meat. Bake at 350° for 20 minutes or until bubbly. Serve with round taco chips.

Braunschweiger Spread

Serves 8

1 8-ounce package
   braunschweiger
1 8-ounce package cream
   cheese
1 tablespoon minced onion
1 tablespoon prepared
   mustard
1 tablespoon Worcester-
   shire sauce

Allow braunschweiger and cream cheese to soften at room temperature. Add onion, mustard and Worcestershire sauce and mix thoroughly. Serve with crackers as a spread, or add a few drops of milk to thin and serve as a dip with chips.

Ham 'n Artichoke Fancies

Makes 20-24 appetizers

1 6-ounce jar marinated
    artichoke hearts,
    drained
3 ounces cream cheese,
    softened
6 4×6″ slices baked or
    boiled ham

Cut artichokes into halves and blot excess moisture with paper towels. Spread cream cheese gen-
erously on ham slices. Place 2 or 3 artichoke pieces
at narrow end of each ham slice. Roll up, jelly roll
fashion. Place ham rolls seam-side down on plate.
Cover and chill. To serve, carefully cut each ham
roll with a serrated knife into ¾″ slices. Secure with
cocktail picks.

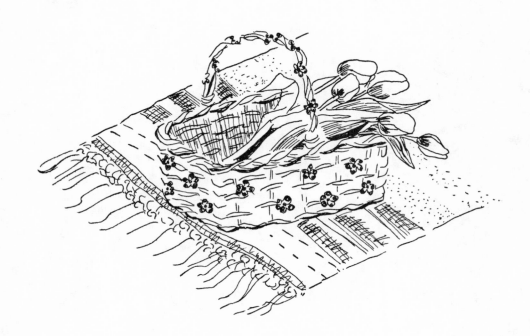

Recipes from Iowa with Love...

Spinach Spread

Serves 4-6

1 **10-ounce package frozen spinach**
2 **tablespoons finely minced green onions**
¼ **cup mayonnaise**
½ **teaspoon lemon juice**
½ **teaspoon Worcestershire sauce**
½ **teaspoon horseradish**
4 **drops red pepper sauce**

Thaw spinach. Squeeze out juice. Mix with remaining ingredients. Cover and refrigerate 6-8 hours. Serve as a spread with whole wheat crackers.

If you're counting calories, substitute yogurt for mayonnaise.

Spinach-Wrapped Chicken with Oriental Dip

Makes 50 pieces

2 **chicken breasts, about
2 pounds**
1 **14-ounce can chicken
broth**
¼ **cup soy sauce**
1 **tablespoon Worcester-
shire sauce**
1 **pound fresh spinach**

Simmer chicken in broth, soy sauce and Worcestershire sauce until tender; about 20 minutes. Remove from broth and cool. Discard skin and bones, and cut meat into 1" chunks. Wash spinach and remove stems. Put spinach in a colander and pour 2-3 quarts boiling water over the leaves. Drain. To assemble, place chicken chunk at stem end of spinach leaf. Roll over once, fold leaf in on both sides and continue rolling around chicken. Chill and serve with wooden picks.

Oriental Dip
½ **cup sour cream**
1 **teaspoon toasted sesame
seeds**
¼ **teaspoon ground ginger**
2 **teaspoons soy sauce**
1 **teaspoon Worcestershire
sauce**

Mix ingredients for Oriental Dip together and chill.

Before the trails were clearly marked, early settlers could wander for days trying to find the way to their destination. A man named Dillon plowed a 100-mile furrow from Dubuque to Iowa City to mark the route between these two settlements. Later, this became a road, and today one of the state highways follows parts of this original trail.

Cheese Artichoke Dip

Serves 8

1 **14-ounce can artichoke hearts, drained and chopped**
1 **6-ounce jar marinated artichoke hearts, drained and chopped**
1 **4-ounce can green chilies, drained and chopped**
6 **tablespoons mayonnaise**
2 **cups grated Cheddar cheese**

Mix ingredients together. Place in au gratin dish or 1½-quart casserole. Bake at 350° for 20 minutes. Serve with crackers.

Recipes from Iowa with Love...

Pigs are extremely bright. Though they are bred for food, they can become delightful pets, and some have been trained as "watch pigs." Breeders today strive for the smaller, lean-meat pig instead of the larger pig of a few years ago.

Crispy Bacon Bites
"easy to do, and really good"

Serves 8

8 very thin bacon slices
16 square stone ground wheat crackers or rectangular saltine crackers

Cut each bacon slice in half. Wrap bacon around cracker, covering cracker. Place on a broiler pan or a rack set inside a rimmed cookie sheet. Bake at 300° until bacon is cooked, about 25 minutes. Parmesan cheese may be sprinkled on tops during last 15 minutes if desired. Cool briefly on rack to crisp bacon and serve warm.

Zucchini squash proliferates in Iowa during the late summer. Iowa cooks whip up zucchini cookies, zucchini bread, zucchini pie and zucchini preserves in an attempt to keep up with the abundance. The following is one delicious solution to "the zucchini problem."

Zucchini Appetizers

"for non-lovers of zucchini"

Makes 48 bars

3 cups zucchini, unpared and thinly sliced
1 cup biscuit mix
½ cup onion, finely chopped
½ cup Parmesan cheese, grated
2 tablespoons parsley, snipped
½ teaspoon salt
½ teaspoon seasoned salt
½ teaspoon dried oregano or marjoram
1 clove garlic, finely chopped
Dash of pepper
½ cup vegetable oil
4 eggs, slightly beaten

Heat oven to 350°. Grease 9×13″ pan. Mix all the ingredients together and spread in pan. Bake 25 minutes or until brown. Cut into 1×2″ pieces.

Recipes from Iowa with Love...

One-Two-Three Sausage Balls

"pastry balls full of cheese and sausage"

Makes 40

1 pound hot bulk sausage
2 cups grated sharp
    Cheddar cheese
3 cups prepared biscuit mix

Mix ingredients together thoroughly. Form into 1" balls and bake at 350° for 20 minutes. May be eaten with or without Mustard Dip.

Mustard Dip

"excellent with crisp vegetables, too"

¾ cup mayonnaise
2 tablespoons prepared
    mustard
⅛ teaspoon Worcestershire
    sauce
½ teaspoon garlic salt

Mix ingredients and refrigerate till ready to serve.

Salmon Puffs

"makings are usually on the pantry shelf"

Makes 30-40

2 cups canned salmon,
    drained, bones and
    skin removed
¾ cup cracker crumbs
    (reserve ¼ cup)
½ small onion, chopped
1 tablespoon lemon juice
2 tablespoons melted
    butter
1 tablespoon pickle relish
1 tablespoon garlic powder
½ teaspoon Worcestershire
    sauce
    Salt and pepper to taste

Mix salmon with ½ cup cracker crumbs. Add remaining ingredients, mix well, and form into 1" balls. Roll in reserved cracker crumbs and bake at 350° for 20 minutes. Serve with Mustard Dip.

Creamy Cucumber Dip

Makes 2 cups

2 large cucumbers,
   chopped fine
1 large onion, chopped fine
1 tablespoon sugar
1 teaspoon salt
   Vinegar
1 8-ounce package cream
   cheese, softened

Mix cucumbers, onion, sugar and salt in mixing bowl. Add enough vinegar to cover. Let stand for 1 hour. Drain and press out moisture. Beat cream cheese with mixer or food processor. Add cucumber mixture and blend until creamy smooth.

Cheese on Party Rye

Makes 1½ cups

3 ounces shredded
   Cheddar cheese
1 small can chopped ripe
   olives
½ cup chopped green onion
½ cup mayonnaise
½ teaspoon curry powder
   Party rye bread

Mix spread ingredients and refrigerate for several hours. Spread on slices of party rye bread and bake at 400° for 3 to 4 minutes.

Recipes from Iowa with Love...

"The surprising place" has become a slogan for Des Moines because so many visitors are surprised by the attractiveness of the city and the number of things available to see and do.

Surprising Meatballs

Makes 24-30 meatballs

1 **pound ground beef**
½ **cup soft bread crumbs**
⅓ **cup minced onion**
¼ **cup milk**
1 **egg**
1 **teaspoon salt**
⅛ **teaspoon pepper**
½ **teaspoon Worcestershire sauce**
½ **cup shortening**
1 **12-ounce bottle chili sauce**
1 **10-ounce jar grape jelly**

Combine beef, crumbs, onion, milk, egg, salt, pepper and Worcestershire sauce. Shape into 1″ balls. Melt shortening in large skillet and brown meatballs. Remove from pan and pour off fat. In skillet, mix chili sauce and jelly, heating gently and stirring until jelly melts. Add meatballs and simmer, uncovered, for 30 minutes. Spoon sauce over meatballs occasionally. Serve in chafing dish with cocktail picks.

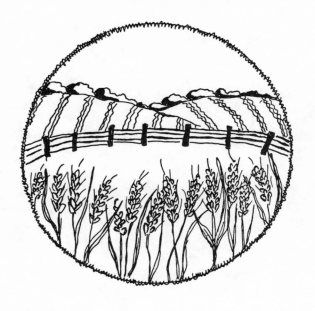

Breads
and
Brunch

Recipes from Iowa with Love...

The city of Council Bluffs derives its name from the high bluffs overlooking the Missouri River, where Lewis and Clark and the Otoe and Missouri Indians conducted a council meeting during the 1804 expedition.

Council Bluffs Apple Pastry Bars
"flaky and delicious"

Makes 20-24 pieces

2½ **cups flour**
1 **teaspoon salt**
1 **cup margarine**
1 **egg yolk**
  Milk
½ **cup crushed corn flakes**
8- 10 **apples, peeled and thinly sliced**
1 **teaspoon cinnamon**
1 **cup granulated sugar**
1 **egg white**
1 **tablespoon water**
1 **cup powdered sugar**
½ **teaspoon vanilla**

Mix flour and salt together; cut in margarine. Mix egg yolk and enough milk to equal ⅔ cup. Gradually combine flour mixture and milk mixture to make a pastry similar to pie dough. Roll out half the dough to fit a 10×15" jelly roll pan or a cookie sheet. Sprinkle bottom crust with crushed cereal. Layer apples over cereal; sprinkle with cinnamon and granulated sugar. Roll remaining dough and place on top of apples, fitting and pinching the edges together. Beat egg white until stiff and brush over crust. Bake at 350° for 50-60 minutes. While still warm, frost with mixture of water, powdered sugar and vanilla.

Spoonbread recipes are found in nearly all the accounts of cooking in the 1800's.

Mable's Spoonbread

"don't slice it...eat it with a spoon"

Serves 8

2 cups water
1 cup corn meal
2 tablespoons butter
½ teaspoon salt
1 tablespoon sugar
1 13-ounce can evaporated
   milk
4 eggs, beaten
3 tablespoons water

Bring 2 cups water to boil, remove from heat. Slowly add corn meal, a little at a time to prevent lumping. Put on low heat, cook for 3 minutes. Add butter, salt and sugar. Continue cooking for 5 minutes. Remove from heat, add evaporated milk, eggs and water. Beat well. Pour into buttered 9×9" casserole. Bake at 350° for 45-60 minutes or until bread "passes clean butter knife test."

Recipes from Iowa with Love...

The first Iowa State Fair was held in Fairfield in 1854. The featured entertainment was an exhibition of women riding horseback. Today, Fairfield is the home of Maharishi International University, which draws students from every corner of the world.

Fairfield Honey Corn Bread

1½ cups stone-ground
      yellow cornmeal
½ cups unbleached flour
½ teaspoon soda
1 cup milk
¼ cup butter, melted
⅓ cup honey

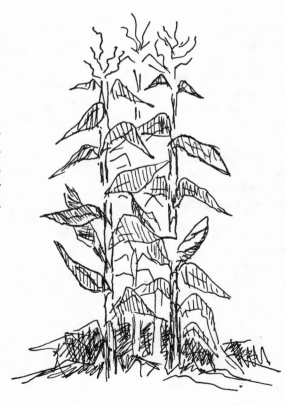

Mix dry ingredients in a blender or food processor. Mix milk, butter and honey together and add to dry ingredients. Pour into a greased 8″ square pan and bake at 425° for 20-25 minutes.

Recipes from Iowa with Love...

Nearly one-fourth of the population of Cedar Rapids is of Czechoslovakian descent, a higher percentage than in any other city in the United States. Spillville, a small town in northeast Iowa, has an even stronger Czech influence. Antonin Dvorak spent a summer in this idyllic setting in 1893, and may have done some of the arrangements for his *New World Symphony* there.

New World Kolaches
"fruit filled buns"

Makes 30

1 teaspoon salt
½ cup sugar
1 cup lukewarm milk
2 packages active dry yeast
2 eggs, beaten
½ cup soft shortening
4-5 cups flour

Prune Filling
1½ cups pitted prunes
4 tablespoons sugar
1 teaspoon cinnamon

Apricot Filling
1½ cups dried apricots
½ cup sugar

Combine salt, sugar and milk. Crumble yeast into the mixture and let stand until it becomes frothy. Mix in eggs, shortening and flour. Turn onto a floured board and knead dough about 10 minutes. Place dough in a greased bowl and let stand in a warm place until doubled in bulk. Punch dough down and let rise again until doubled. Form dough into 2" balls and let rise until doubled. Press an indentation in each ball and fill with fruit filling. Bake at 400° for 20 minutes.

To make fruit filling, cook fruit in small amount of water, cool and mash or puree in the blender. Add sugar to fruit, and if making prune filling, add cinnamon.

Recipes from Iowa with Love...

Even while living in sod huts, Iowa's early pioneer women maintained some of the rituals of more gracious living. Accounts of frontier social calls nearly always mention that tea and biscuits were served.

Sweet Tea Biscuits

Makes 2 dozen

½ cup milk
1 cup sugar
1 teaspoon soda
3¼ cups sifted flour
¾ cup quick or old-
    fashioned oats
½ teaspoon salt
1 cup soft butter or
    margarine

Place milk and sugar in a saucepan and bring to a boil. Remove from heat. Add soda, stirring to dissolve. Combine flour, oats and salt in bowl. Cut in butter until mixture resembles coarse crumbs. Add milk mixture and stir to moisten dry ingredients. Turn out on lightly floured board. Knead 10 times; roll out to ⅓-inch thickness. Cut with floured 2½-inch round biscuit cutter. Place on ungreased cookie sheet and bake at 400° 10-12 minutes. Serve with butter and marmalade.

Oatmeal Bread

Makes 2 loaves

1½ **cups boiling water**
1 **cup rolled oats**
¾ **cup molasses**
3 **tablespoons butter**
2 **teaspoons salt**
1 **tablespoon dry yeast**
2 **cups lukewarm water**
7-8 **cups unbleached flour**
Butter

Pour boiling water over oats and let stand 30 minutes. Add molasses, butter and salt. Sprinkle yeast on lukewarm water; stir to dissolve. Add to oats mixture. Add 2 cups flour, beat with electric mixer at medium speed until smooth. Gradually add enough remaining flour to make medium soft dough. Turn onto floured board and knead 10 minutes. Place dough in lightly greased bowl; turn over to grease top. Cover with damp cloth and let rise in warm place until doubled. Knead again for 2 minutes. Divide in half, shape and place in 2 greased 9×5" loaf pans. Let rise until doubled. Bake at 400° for 5 minutes, lower heat to 350° and bake another 45 minutes. Remove from pans, cool on racks. Brush tops with butter while still hot.

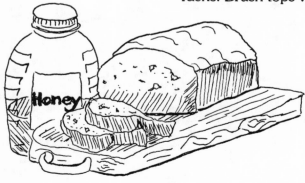

Whole Wheat Bran Muffins
"full of good things"

Makes 1 dozen muffins

2 tablespoons oil
½ cup honey or molasses
1 egg, beaten
¾ cup milk
1½ cups bran
1 cup whole wheat flour
1 teaspoon soda
1 teaspoon baking powder
½ cup raisins

Mix oil and honey together and add egg. Beat well. Stir in milk and bran. Sift flour, soda, and baking powder together and stir into egg mixture until moistened. Add raisins and mix briefly. Fill greased muffin tins ⅔ full and bake at 425° for 20-25 minutes.

Herbert Hoover, 31st President of the United States, was born at West Branch. The two-room cottage where he was born and the Presidential Library are part of the Herbert Hoover National Historic site located there. In a speech in 1927 he was reminiscing about food in Iowa and stated "if all the cooks in Iowa are up to Aunt Millie's standard, then the gourmets of the world should leave Paris for Iowa..."

Zucchini Bread

"it's not Aunt Millie's, but it's good"

Makes 4 small loaves

3 eggs
1 cup oil
1/3 cup packed brown sugar
2 cups grated zucchini
2 teaspoons vanilla
1 2/3 cups granulated sugar
3 cups flour
1 teaspoon soda
1/4 teaspoon baking powder
1 teaspoon salt
2 teaspoons cinnamon

Beat eggs until foamy. Add oil, brown sugar, zucchini, vanilla and granulated sugar. Mix lightly. Sift together flour, soda, baking powder, salt and cinnamon. Add to the egg mixture and blend. Pour mixture into 4 small loaf pans. Bake at 325° for 1 hour or until done.

Recipes from Iowa with Love...

Onion Cheese Bread

Serves 8

½ cup chopped onion
2 tablespoons butter
½ cup milk
1 egg, beaten
1½ cups biscuit mix
1 cup shredded Cheddar
   cheese
2 teaspoons parsley flakes

Saute onion lightly in butter. Set aside. Combine milk and egg, and add biscuit mix. Stir only enough to moisten; add cooked onion, ½ cup cheese and the parsley. Pour into 8" square pan and sprinkle with the other ½ cup cheese. Bake at 400° for 20 minutes or until done. This is best served warm.

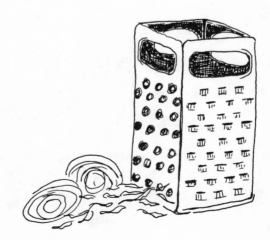

Banana Bread
"moist and rich with lots of flavor"

Makes 2 loaves

1¼ cups sugar
 ½ cup shortening
  2 eggs
  2 tablespoons sour cream
2½ cups sifted flour
  1 teaspoon soda
  1 teaspoon baking powder
 ½ teaspoon salt
  3 large very ripe bananas, mashed
 ½ cup nuts, chopped

Cream sugar and shortening together; add eggs one at a time, beating after each. Add sour cream. Sift dry ingredients together and add to egg mixture alternating with the bananas. Fold in nuts. Bake in 2 greased loaf pans at 325° for about 45-55 minutes. Test with wooden pick to determine if done. Allow to cool 30 minutes before removing from pan.

Recipes from Iowa with Love...

In 1889, the University of Iowa and Grinnell College met in the first intercollegiate football game ever played west of the Mississippi.

Breakfast Supreme

"perfect for a relaxed weekend brunch"

Serves 4-6

4 slices white bread, crusts removed
1 package brown-and-serve sausage, cubed
½ pound grated Cheddar cheese
4 eggs, beaten
½ teaspoon dry mustard
2 cups milk
Salt and pepper

Cut bread into cubes and spread in bottom of an oiled 9×13" baking dish. Cover with meat and cheese. Mix eggs, mustard, milk, salt and pepper; pour over meat and cheese. Refrigerate overnight and bake at 300° for 1 hour.

Creamy Scrambled Eggs with Sprouts

Serves 2

1½ tablespoons butter
½ cup bean sprouts
½ cup cottage cheese, drained
¼ teaspoon salt
Freshly ground pepper to taste
4 eggs

Melt butter in skillet over medium low heat. Add sprouts, cottage cheese, salt and pepper; mix. Break the eggs into the skillet and stir with fork until set.

The Mesquakie Indians were moved from their home in Iowa to a reservation in Kansas in the 1840's. One day, their chiefs came to Iowa's Governor Grimes with a bag of money, which they placed on his desk. They had saved their cash over a period of time, and wanted to buy land so they could return to their beloved Iowa. Today, they own a large tract of land near Tama and are proud of their independence.

Indian Fry Bread

Makes 12 pieces

2 cups flour
3¼ teaspoons baking powder
½ teaspoon salt
1 cup water, medium hot
1 pound lard

Mix ingredients except lard together thoroughly. On a slightly floured board, roll until ½" thick. Cut into 3" round patties. Form with hands until shape is like a flattened ball. Heat lard in a deep skillet until it begins to smoke. Drop balls of dough into lard and cook until golden brown. Drain on paper towels. Serve with honey or apple butter.

Esther's Cream Cheese Blintzes

"finger food for a brunch"

Serves 6

12 slices white bread
1 8-ounce package cream cheese, softened
1 teaspoon milk
½ cup melted butter
2 teaspoons cinnamon
2 tablespoons sugar

Cut crusts off bread and, using a rolling pin, roll each slice thin. Mix cream cheese and milk, and spread on bread slices. Roll up bread and cheese and cut into thirds. Dip in melted butter, then into cinnamon-sugar mixture. Bake at 350° for 12-15 minutes.

Buttermilk Waffles

Makes 8

3 eggs
1½ cups buttermilk or
       sour milk
1 teaspoon soda
1¾ cups flour
2 teaspoons baking powder
½ teaspoon salt
½ cup oil

Beat eggs in a medium mixing bowl. Add buttermilk. Sift soda, flour, baking powder and salt together. Stir into the buttermilk mixture. Add oil and beat. This will be a thin batter. Bake on a hot waffle iron until waffles stop steaming.

Soups
and
Salads

Cream of Asparagus Soup

Serves 4-6

3 tablespoons butter
½ cup chopped green onions
1 clove garlic, minced
2 pounds asparagus
   (reserve some of
   the tips)
1 teaspoon lemon juice
3-4 cups chicken broth
1 tablespoon chopped
   parsley
   Salt and pepper to taste
½ teaspoon tarragon
1- 1½ cups light cream

Melt butter in saucepan over low heat and add green onions, garlic, asparagus and lemon juice and cook for 5 minutes. Add chicken broth to cover and parsley. Cook slowly until asparagus is soft. Put through food mill or blender, sieve and return to saucepan. Add salt, pepper, and tarragon. Add more chicken broth to taste and reserved asparagus tips. Simmer 2 minutes; add cream, heat thoroughly and serve.

Italian Hot Sausage Soup
"a hearty meal on a cold winter night"

Serves 10

1½ pounds Italian hot sausage
1 28-ounce can Italian
   pear shaped tomatoes
3 14½-ounce cans chicken
   broth
1 large onion, thinly sliced
1 medium zucchini, thinly
   sliced and slices
   quartered
1 large green pepper,
   thinly sliced
2 tablespoons olive oil
¼ teaspoon oregano
1 bay leaf
   Pinch of thyme
   Salt and pepper to taste
¾ cup uncooked bow shaped
   pasta
1½ cups red wine

Fry Italian sausage till done. Pour off grease and slice into ½-inch slices. Add remaining ingredients except pasta and red wine. Cover and simmer 20 minutes. Add pasta and red wine, cover and simmer another 20 minutes.

Recipes from Iowa with Love...

A tradition of one fine Des Moines hostess is to have a Groundhog Party every February 2nd. The first time we received an invitation for groundhog soup, it took a moment...to get the connection between "ground hog" and sausage.

Jo's Groundhog Soup
"delicious on February 2 and every other day"

Serves 8

1 **pound bulk sausage**
1 **large onion, chopped**
½ **cup chopped green pepper**
1 **large can tomatoes**
2 **15-ounce cans kidney beans, drained and rinsed**
1 **quart water**
1 **bay leaf**
1½ **teaspoons salt**
½ **teaspoon garlic salt**
½ **teaspoon thyme**
Ground pepper to taste
1 **cup diced potatoes**

Brown sausage in large skillet. Add onion and green pepper and cook until tender. Drain excess drippings. Add tomatoes, beans, water and seasonings. Cook covered for 2 hours, add potatoes and continue cooking until potatoes are tender.

Creamy Broccoli Soup

Serves 6-8

2 tablespoons minced
    onion
3 tablespoons butter or
    margarine
3 tablespoons flour
1½ teaspoons salt
3 cups chicken broth
2 cups fresh broccoli,
    chopped; or 1 10-ounce
    package frozen
    chopped broccoli
2 cups thinly sliced carrots
3 cups milk
    Salt and pepper to taste

Saute onion in butter until tender; stir in flour and salt. Add broth, stirring constantly. Add broccoli and carrots and simmer 20 minutes or until carrots are tender. Add milk and salt and pepper to taste. Heat and serve.

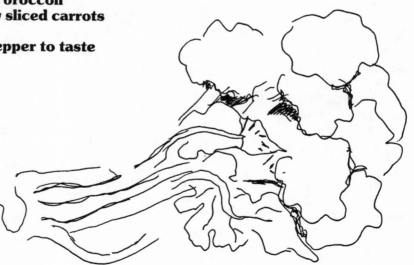

"Oh we're from Ioway, Ioway..." The words to the rousing Iowa Corn Song were written by two Des Moines Shriners, George Hamilton and John Beeston, while they were on their way to a Shrine convention in California in 1921. They adapted the lyrics to a popular tune of the times. While it has never had any official recognition, it is the most widely known song about Iowa.

Cream of Corn Soup

Serves 4-6

2   slices bacon, finely diced
2   tablespoons onion,
    chopped fine
2   cups frozen or fresh
    corn, cut off cob
2   tablespoons butter
2   tablespoons flour
2   cups milk
1   teaspoon salt
¼   teaspoon pepper
2   cups light cream

Fry bacon until crisp. Add onion and saute until soft. Add corn to bacon and onion and cook until corn begins to brown. Add butter, stir till melted and add flour. Cook for 3 minutes. Add milk, salt and pepper and cook until thickened. Add light cream and heat thoroughly.

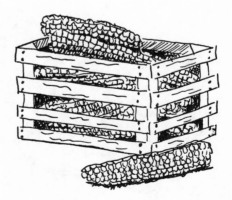

Dubuque, Iowa's oldest city, was founded in 1788 when a French entre-preneur, Julien Dubuque, began mining lead in the area. The city has been ruled under the flags of five nations: France, Spain, Napoleon's France, England and the United States.

French Pea Soup

"this has a lovely fresh flavor, and is good either hot or cold"

Serves 4-5

3 cups chicken broth
1 medium carrot, peeled and diced
1 teaspoon chervil or chopped parsley
1 10-ounce package frozen petite peas, thawed
2 tablespoons melted butter or margarine
   Salt and pepper to taste

Bring chicken broth, carrot and chervil or parsley to boil in medium saucepan. Reduce heat, cover and simmer 5 minutes or until carrot is tender. Transfer mixture to blender. Add thawed peas and butter and blend until smoothly pureed. Stir in salt and pepper to taste.

"Go west, young man; go west and grow up with the country." This advice was given to Josiah Grinnell by the publisher, Horace Greeley. Grinnell, who was a Congregational minister, took his advice and became one of the founders of a settlement which is now the town of Grinnell. Grinnell College, one of the nation's finest liberal arts colleges, is located there.

Grinnell Zucchini Soup

"whip in the blender; it's smooth and green and low-caloried"

Serves 4

1 cup chopped onion
1 cup chopped green
   pepper
1 tablespoon oil or butter
6 cups zucchini, unpeeled
   and cut into 1" chunks
1-2 cloves garlic, minced
2 14-ounce cans chicken
   broth
1 teaspoon salt
¼ teaspoon pepper
¼ cup chopped parsley
1 scant teaspoon oregano
1 cup water
1 tablespoon chopped
   chives

Saute onion and green pepper in butter or oil until tender. Add remaining ingredients, except chives, and cook 10 minutes. Pour into blender and puree for 30 seconds. Serve hot, garnished with finely chopped chives. Freezes well.

During the football season, fans of the University of Iowa Hawkeyes and the Iowa State University Cyclones gather in Iowa City and Ames to cheer their respective teams. An important part of these events is the tailgating that precedes the games. The food for these parking lot parties ranges from basic sandwiches to elaborate gourmet fare.

Mostaccioli Salad

"great pasta salad for a tailgate take-along"

Serves 6-8

8 ounces mostaccioli, cooked
½ cup chopped onions
⅓ cup pickle relish
½ small jar pimentos (optional)
1 cup mayonnaise-type salad dressing
½ teaspoon garlic powder
½ teaspoon celery salt
¼ teaspoon oregano
Salt and pepper to taste

Mix all ingredients together and refrigerate at least 4 hours.

Recipes from Iowa with Love...

During the 1840's, thousands of Mormans crossed Iowa on their move from Illinois to Utah. These Morman trails became the early roads for other settlers who came later.

Spaghetti Salad

Serves 12

1 pound thin spaghetti
½ cucumber, chopped fine
6 radishes, sliced fine
1 bunch green onions, sliced
1½ teaspoons salt
1 teaspoon sugar
¾ teaspoon pepper
½ teaspoon celery salt
¼ teaspoon oregano
4 hard-cooked eggs, chopped

Break spaghetti into 3-inch pieces and cook according to package directions. Drain, and add remaining ingredients. Cool. Toss with Dressing.

Dressing
3 cups mayonnaise
½ cup sour cream
¾ cup light cream
3 tablespoons Durkee's sauce
1½ teaspoon Dijon mustard

Mix dressing ingredients together and add to spaghetti mixture. Cover and refrigerate overnight.

Caroline's Cabbage Slaw
"allow 24 hours for flavors to blend"

Serves 8

1 large head of cabbage
2 onions, finely chopped
2 carrots, finely chopped
1 green pepper, finely
   chopped
½ sweet red pepper
   (optional)
6 stuffed olives, sliced

Slice cabbage very fine with a sharp knife. Combine with remaining ingredients. Toss with hot dressing.

Hot Dressing
1 cup white vinegar
1 cup sugar
½ cup oil
1 teaspoon salt
1 teaspoon celery seed
1 teaspoon dry mustard
½ clove garlic, minced

Combine all ingredients in small saucepan and bring to a boil. Lower heat and simmer about 3 minutes. Pour over cabbage. Cool, and refrigerate at least 24 hours, stirring occasionally. Keeps well and gets better the longer it sits in the refrigerator.

Shoe Peg Corn Salad
"a vegetable salad that tastes like a fresh, crisp relish"

Serves 12

1 cup diced celery
1 cup diced green pepper
¼ cup diced onion
1 2-ounce jar pimentos, diced
1 1-pound can sliced green beans, drained
1 1-pound can white shoe peg corn, drained
1 1-pound can tiny peas
¼ cup oil
¾ cup white vinegar
1 cup sugar

Combine vegetables in large bowl. Mix oil, vinegar and sugar together and pour over vegetables. Mix and refrigerate 24 hours before serving.

Recipes from Iowa with Love...

The LeGrand limestone quarries in Marshall County provide important clues to prehistoric life in Iowa. One of Iowa's famous native archaeologists, B. H. Beane, has discovered and preserved hundreds of fossilized star fish, sea lilies and other animals which lived in this inland sea 300 million years ago.

Marshall Bean Salad

"Italian green beans and ripe olives"

Serves 6-8

1 9-ounce package frozen
   Italian green beans
½ cup Italian salad dressing
½ cup mayonnaise
1 16-ounce can red kidney
   beans, drained
1 7-ounce can pitted ripe
   olives, sliced
1 cup celery
1 small red onion,
   thinly sliced

Steam frozen Italian beans until crisply tender, drain, and allow to cool. Mix salad dressing into mayonnaise until smooth. Mix in beans and remaining ingredients. Toss lightly and chill at least 4 hours.

Historians are not sure of the meaning of the word "Iowa." Our state was named for the Ioway Indians, and we have taken to our hearts the explanation that Ioway comes from a French-Indian word meaning "beautiful land."

Beautiful Land Salad

"crunchy vegetables marinated in a dill dressing"

Serves 8

1 small head cauliflower
1 10-ounce package frozen artichoke hearts, cooked
½ cup chopped onion
½ cup chopped celery
⅔ cup mayonnaise
2 tablespoons chili sauce
2 teaspoons lemon juice
2 teaspoons dill weed
1 teaspoon salt
   Salad greens

Break cauliflower into flowerets and slice into bite-size pieces. Slice artichoke hearts and add onion and celery. Mix remaining ingredients except greens and pour half of mixture over vegetables. Marinate overnight. When ready to serve, toss with remaining half of dressing. Serve on a bed of salad greens.

Des Moines has been called "The Hartford of the West" because it is a major insurance center. In 1980, there were 49 multiple line insurance companies and 35 life insurance companies with corporation headquarters in the capital city.

Cucumber Ring

Serves 6

½ cup cold water
1 envelope unflavored
   gelatin
½ teaspoon salt
1 large cucumber
3 cups creamed cottage
   cheese, drained
8 ounces cream cheese
2 tablespoons grated onion
½ cup mayonnaise
⅔ cup celery, chopped fine
½ cup chopped nuts

Stir water into gelatin slowly; add salt and stir over low heat until gelatin is dissolved. Cut cucumber in half, scrape out seeds and grate. Squeeze out excess moisture. You should have ¾ to 1 cup grated cucumber. Beat cottage cheese and cream cheese together. Add cucumber, gelatin, onion and remaining ingredients. Spoon into 6-cup mold and chill 6 hours.

Garden Souffle Salad

Serves 10

2 large packages lemon
   gelatin
3 cups hot water
3 tablespoons vinegar
½ teaspoon salt
⅛ teaspoon pepper
1 cup mayonnaise
2 tablespoons grated onion
1 teaspoon diced green
   pepper
¾ cup diced cauliflower
¾ cup shredded carrots
¾ cup diced celery
¾ cup sliced radishes

Dissolve gelatin in hot water. Add vinegar, salt, pepper and mayonnaise; stir until mixed. Chill till thickened. Beat with an electric mixer at low speed until fluffy. Fold in the vegetables and put in a 2-quart dish or mold. Chill and serve.

Meredith Willson wrote his hit play *The Music Man* about Mason City in 1912. His musical career began when he learned to play the flute for the high school band. During the 1940's, he wrote the song "*Iowa*," which became the centennial song in 1946.

Apricot-Pineapple Salad
"real fruit flavor with a creamy topping"

Serves 12

1 3-ounce package lemon
    gelatin
1 3-ounce package orange
    gelatin
2 cups boiling water
1 16-ounce can crushed
    pineapple
1 16-ounce can apricots
1 cup fruit juice, drained
    from cans of fruit

Mix gelatin with boiling water and stir until dissolved. Drain pineapple and apricots, reserving juice. Puree apricots in blender or sieve. Mix fruit into gelatin and add fruit juice. Pour into lightly oiled 9×13" glass baking dish. Refrigerate until set.

Topping
½ cup sugar
1 tablespoon flour
1 egg, beaten
1 cup fruit juice, drained
    from cans of fruit and
    orange juice
2 tablespoons butter
1 cup whipping cream,
    whipped
½ cup grated Longhorn or
    Cheddar cheese

Cook sugar, flour, egg and fruit juice until thick. Remove from heat and stir in butter. Cool. Fold in whipped cream and spread over the gelatin layer. Top with grated cheese.

Recipes from Iowa with Love...

The bridge over Honey Creek near Ogden was washed out by a raging storm and flood on a July night in 1881. Fifteen-year old Kate Shelley braved the storm, crawled across the wooden ties of the railroad bridge over the Des Moines River, and flagged down the scheduled passenger train to warn of the danger ahead. The lantern she carried that night is on display in the State Historical Building.

Honey-Avocado Fruit Dressing

"can be used as a dip or a dressing"

2 ripe avocados, peeled
⅓ cup honey
⅓ cup orange juice
1 cup whipping cream

Puree avocados 15 seconds in blender or food processor. Blend in honey and orange juice. Whip the cream until it forms peaks and fold in the avocado mixture. Serve surrounded by fresh fruit such as strawberries, melons, apples, and pears; cut into wedges, chunks and bite-sized pieces.

Sunny Salad

Serves 6

1 bunch broccoli, cut in
   bite-size pieces
½ pound bacon, fried and
   crumbled
½ cup sunflower seeds
½ cup raisins
4 tablespoons minced
   onions

   Marinade
½ cup mayonnaise
2 tablespoons vinegar
2 tablespoons sugar
4 teaspoons milk

Toss salad ingredients with marinade dressing at least 2 hours before serving. The longer the flavors blend, the better.

Recipes from Iowa with Love...

Bean sprouts have been important in the Chinese diet for centuries. They are one of the most concentrated and nutritious foods known to man.

Fresh Spinach and Sesame Seed Salad

"this is a four-star salad...wonderful"

Serves 6-8

½ **pound fresh mushrooms, washed and dried**
½ **cup bottled Italian salad dressing**
1 **pound fresh spinach, washed carefully**
1½ **cups fresh bean sprouts**
⅓ **cup oil**
3 **tablespoons lemon juice**
2 **tablespoons soy sauce**
¼ **teaspoon salt**
2 **tablespoons sesame seeds, toasted**
6 **slices bacon, cooked crisp**

Marinate mushrooms in salad dressing for 1 hour. Remove stems and heavy veins from spinach, using only tender leaves. Combine spinach, sprouts, and marinated mushrooms. Combine oil, lemon juice, soy sauce, salt and sesame seeds; pour over the mixture. Crumble bacon and sprinkle on top. Toss and serve.

We talk a lot about weather in Iowa because it is so changeable. The warm air from the gulf, the cold winds from Canada and the turbulence from the Rocky Mountains come together in our state. For people who like the changing seasons, Iowa is the place to be. It is hot in the summer, cold in the winter, full of surprises in the spring and beautiful in the fall.

Cobb Salad

"a beautiful salad for a summer buffet"

Serves 6

1 head iceberg lettuce
1 bunch watercress
½ head romaine lettuce
2 tablespoons minced chives
3 medium tomatoes, peeled, seeded and diced
6 slices bacon, cooked
2 cups cooked chicken breast, cut into bite-size cubes
3 hard-cooked eggs, diced
2 avocados, peeled and diced
1 teaspoon lemon juice
French dressing

Finely shred iceberg lettuce, half of watercress, romaine and chives. Toss together and line a large, flat salad bowl. Make separate strips across greens with tomatoes, crumbled bacon, chicken, eggs, and avocados sprinkled with lemon juice. Sprinkle the rest of the watercress over the top, and drizzle French dressing on the salad. Do not toss, but pass additional dressing.

Clear Lake was a favorite camping spot of the Sioux and Winnebago Indians when they were not battling each other. Today it is the favorite summer vacation area of thousands of Iowans.

Clear Lake Salad
"vary the vegetables to fit your preference"

Serves 6-8

Marinade
1 cup salad oil
½ cup wine vinegar
1 garlic bud, pressed
2 tablespoons water
2 tablespoons sugar

1 cup cauliflower, broken
    into bite-size pieces
1 cup sliced fresh
    mushrooms
1 cup green pepper rings
½ cup sliced celery
½ cup broccoli spears,
    sliced into bite-size
    pieces
½ cup sliced cucumbers
½ cup sliced green onions
1 bunch radishes, whole
1 cup cherry tomatoes,
    whole
  Several large lettuce
    leaves

Mix ingredients of marinade together. Mix vegetables in a large bowl and pour marinade over them. Stir gently to coat thoroughly. Allow to marinate for 4-5 hours, stirring occasionally. Arrange lettuce leaves on large platter and arrange drained vegetables on top. Cover sparingly with your favorite Thousand Island Dressing.

Green and White Toss
"crisp and crunchy"

Serves 8

1 pound fresh spinach
1 head romaine lettuce
1 head iceberg lettuce
1 cup sliced fresh
    mushrooms
1 cup sliced celery
1 sliced cauliflower
½ cup sliced green onions
    Salt and pepper, freshly
    ground

Several hours before serving, wash spinach and lettuce. Shake or blot to remove as much water as possible. Remove stems from spinach. Cover and chill greens. Place vegetables in large bowl with the chilled greens. Toss with your favorite oil and vinegar dressing, or with the Deluxe French Dressing.

Deluxe French Dressing

1 cup oil
¼ cup vinegar
1 tablespoon brown sugar
1 tablespoon ketchup
½ teaspoon salt
¼ teaspoon dry mustard
1 teaspoon grated onion
1 clove garlic, crushed

Mix ingredients and allow to blend several hours before serving.

Bill Reichardt's Best-Dressed Salad
"always in good taste"

Serves 8

2 heads romaine lettuce
2 medium tomatoes,
   chopped
1 2-ounce jar pimentos,
   chopped and drained
1 7-ounce can hearts of
   palm, drained and
   sliced
1 6-ounce jar artichoke
   hearts, drained and
   sliced
1 medium red onion, sliced
6 tablespoons olive oil
2 tablespoons red wine
   vinegar, with garlic
Salt and freshly ground
   black pepper, to taste
1 cup freshly grated
   Parmesan cheese

Several hours before serving, separate romaine, wash and drain thoroughly. Refrigerate. When ready to serve, tear bite-size pieces of lettuce into bowl. Add tomatoes, pimentos, hearts of palm, artichoke hearts and onion. Drizzle olive oil over salad, add vinegar, salt and pepper, and toss. Add Parmesan cheese and toss again.

An old Indian legend tells how the Wapsipinicon River got its name. Wapsi, a beautiful maiden, fell in love with Pinicon, the son of an enemy chief. Because they could never marry, the two lovers jumped into the river at the spot of their secret rendevous. Even today, their voices can be heard in the murmuring ripples of the river's current. However, the less romantic-minded say the river was named for a variety of white artichoke that grew along its banks.

Wapsipinicon Salad

Serves 6-8

¼ cup oil
2 tablespoons salad vinegar
1 teaspoon Worcester-
   shire sauce
½ teaspoon salt
1 tablespoon parsley,
   chopped
1 15-ounce can artichoke
   hearts, drained and
   sliced
2 large pink grapefruit,
   sectioned
6 cups salad greens,
   washed and crisped,
   (spinach, romaine,
   iceberg or leaf lettuce)

Combine all of the dressing ingredients, mix and pour over the artichoke hearts. Allow to stand several hours. Peel and section grapefruit with sharp knife so that membrane is removed. Combine with greens, artichokes and dressing; toss gently but thoroughly.

Wheat did not grow well in the Great Plains until the Mennonites immigrated to the Midwest and brought with them a seed-wheat called Turkey Red. It had been grown in Russia and was adapted to the cold winters.

Cracked Wheat Salad (Tabouli)

Serves 4

¾ cup cracked wheat
    (bulgar)
1½ cups snipped parsley
 3 medium tomatoes,
    chopped
⅓ cup chopped green onions
 2 tablespoons fresh mint
    (or 2 teaspoons dried)
¼ cup olive oil
¼ cup lemon juice
 1 teaspoon salt
    Ripe olives

Cover the wheat with cold water and let stand for 30 minutes. Drain and squeeze water from wheat thoroughly. Place all the ingredients in a glass bowl and toss well. Cover and chill for several hours. Garnish with ripe olives.

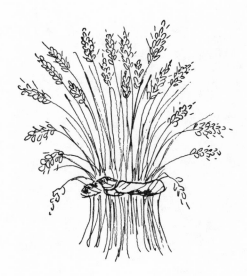

Main
Dishes

Recipes from Iowa with Love...

Valley Junction was the junction of two railroad lines when it was named in 1893. It later became West Des Moines, but the downtown area, with its many antique shops, art galleries and crafts stores still uses the Valley Junction name and retains the flavor of earlier days.

Valley Junction Stew

"this recipe is at least 80 years old, and still a favorite"

Serves 8-10

5 bacon slices, diced
1 stewing chicken, 4-5 pounds
1 green pepper, chopped
3 pounds canned tomatoes
3 pounds potatoes, peeled and sliced
1 tablespoon salt
6 medium onions, chopped
1 cup sliced celery
24 ounces corn
3 cups water
¼ teaspoon pepper

Fry bacon in a large kettle. Add remaining ingredients and simmer for 1 hour. Remove chicken and allow it to cool until it can be handled. Remove bones and skin, dice meat and return to kettle. Cover and let simmer for 3 hours. If necessary, add more liquid.

Sesame Chicken
"baked chicken breasts with an Oriental touch"

Serves 6-8

1 cup oil
4 cloves garlic, minced
1 tablespoon lemon juice
½ cup soy sauce
2 teaspoons ginger
1 teaspoon monosodium
   glutamate
8 chicken breasts
¾ cup sesame seeds

Mix all ingredients together except chicken and sesame seeds. Place chicken breasts in bowl; pour mixture over them, and marinate for 1 hour. Remove from marinade. Coat with sesame seeds and drizzle marinade over the top. Bake for 1 hour at 350°, basting with marinade every 15 minutes.

Recipes from Iowa with Love...

Lake Okoboji in Northwest Iowa is recognized as one of the three most beautiful blue water lakes in the world according to the National Geographic Society. The other two are Lake Louise in Canada and Lake Geneva in Switzerland.

Okoboji Chicken Casserole

"this recipe always brings compliments"

Serves 8-10

3 cups cooked rice
3 cups cooked chicken breast, cut in 1-inch chunks
1 can cream of chicken soup
1 cup chopped celery
1 cup mayonnaise
1 tablespoon grated onion
1 tablespoon lemon juice
3 hard-cooked eggs, chopped
1 8-ounce can water chestnuts, sliced
1 cup crushed corn flakes
½ cup sliced almonds
2 tablespoons butter, melted

Layer rice in bottom of 9×13" baking pan or 3-quart casserole. Spread chicken evenly over rice. Mix next 7 ingredients and spread over chicken. Mix corn flakes, almonds and butter and spread over the top. Bake at 350° for 40 minutes.

Recipes from Iowa with Love...

Lillian Russell, who was born in Clinton, Iowa, was considered the most beautiful woman in America during the Gay Nineties. She believed that large quantities of green onions and cold showers would help delay the effects of age. She was still acclaimed for her beauty when she was nearly 60, so we've included a few recipes that call for green onions.

Lillian's Chicken Salad

"served at a recent luncheon to enthusiastic compliments"

Serves 8

1 package chicken-
    flavored Rice-A-Roni
6 green onions, sliced
½ cup finely chopped
    green pepper
¼ cup sliced stuffed
    green olives
⅓ cup mayonnaise
2 6-ounce jars artichoke
    hearts, drained
    (save marinade)
¼ teaspoon curry powder
2½ cups cooked chicken
    cut into chunks
    Parsley

Prepare Rice-A-Roni according to directions on box, without using butter. Drain and combine with onions, green pepper and olives. Mix the mayonnaise, marinade from artichokes and curry powder; add to rice mixture. Stir only enough to mix. Add the chicken and artichoke hearts and toss lightly. Chill and serve garnished with parsley.

Recipes from Iowa with Love...

Indianola is the site of the U. S. National Hot Air Balloon Championship competition. It is worth getting up at dawn to watch dozens and dozens of these beautiful balloons rising to begin their flight over the lush farm land below.

Miracle Chicken
"chicken breasts baked in a quiche"

Serves 4

2 **chicken breasts, split, boned and skinned**
2 **tablespoons flour**
1 **egg, beaten**
1 **cup dry bread crumbs, rolled fine**
4 **teaspoons butter**
1 **6-ounce can ripe olives, drained and sliced**
2 **cups shredded Swiss cheese**
3 **tablespoons mayonnaise-style salad dressing**
6 **eggs, beaten**

Dust chicken with flour. Dip in egg and roll in bread crumbs. Place chicken in oiled casserole and top each piece with 1 teaspoon butter. Bake uncovered at 350° for 15-20 minutes or until light brown. Mix olives, cheese, salad dressing and eggs and pour mixture over chicken breasts. Bake uncovered at 350° for an additional 20-25 minutes, or until eggs puff and brown on top.

Recipes from Iowa with Love...

Cheesy Chicken and Ham Bundles
"an elegant recipe... both in taste and appearance"

Serves 6

3 **whole chicken breasts, split**
½ **cup dry sherry (or water)**
3 **bouillon cubes**
2½ **cups hot water**
6 **tablespoons mustard**
¾ **teaspoon garlic salt**
¾ **teaspoon fines herbes (or ¼ teaspoon each sage leaves, basil and thyme)**
6 **slices (4×6") Monterey Jack cheese**
6 **slices (4×6") cooked ham**
1 **10-ounce package frozen patty shells**
1 **egg white, beaten**
1 **tablespoon sesame seed**

Place chicken breasts, sherry, and bouillon, dissolved in water, in large saucepan and bring to a boil. Reduce heat and cover, simmering 30 minutes or until tender when pierced. Let cool in broth; then carefully pull the bone and skin away from breast. Refrigerate chicken to cool completely. Mix together mustard, garlic salt and herbs, then use to thoroughly coat each chicken piece. Wrap a slice of cheese and ham around each. Meanwhile, let patty shells thaw at room temperature for 30 minutes. On a lightly floured board, roll each shell into an 8-inch circle. Place wrapped chicken, seam-side down in center of circle; bring sides up to overlap, moisten and pinch to seal. Place bundles, seam-side down, on ungreased cookie sheet. Brush with egg white; sprinkle with sesame seed and chill for 30 minutes. Bake in a 425° oven for 30 minutes or until richly browned. May be served warm or cold.

Recipes from Iowa with Love...

Pella was once called Strawtown because the early Dutch settlers built their homes of straw and mud. One Dutch woman, upon finding that her precious Delft china had been shattered on the difficult trek westward, refused to give up this last symbol of refinement. Although her house was made of straw, her front walk was paved with tiny shards of broken Delft china.

Borst Van Kip Supreme

"chicken breasts as prepared at the Strawtown Inn in Pella"

Serves 4

4 **whole chicken breasts, skinned and boned**
2 **tablespoons butter**
1 **tablespoon butter**
¾ **cup sliced fresh mushrooms**
1 **tablespoon chopped green onions**
1 **cup heavy cream**
   Salt and pepper to taste
1 **tablespoon brandy**

Cook chicken breasts in 2 tablespoons butter in heavy skillet until they are done and a light golden brown. Meanwhile, heat 1 tablespoon butter in medium skillet, saute mushrooms and onions until tender. Add cream and simmer until sauce thickens. Salt and pepper to taste. When chicken is done pour brandy over it, flame and allow to cook until flame is out. Add sauce and simmer 2-3 minutes.

Iowa has always given highest priority to its "seminaries of learning." The state has three state universities, 28 private four-year colleges and 15 area community colleges and vocational schools. Iowa has the highest literacy rate in the nation.

As You Like It Chicken Breasts

Serves 8

½ pint sour cream
2 tablespoons lemon juice
2 tablespoons Worcester-
    shire sauce
½ cup melted butter
1 teaspoon celery salt
½ teaspoon garlic salt
½ teaspoon salt
    Dash of pepper
8 chicken breasts,
    boned and skinned
3 cups herb seasoned
    stuffing mix, rolled fine

Combine sour cream, lemon juice, Worcestershire sauce and melted butter with seasonings. Dip the chicken breasts in the mixture, then roll them in the stuffing crumbs. Arrange chicken in shallow greased pan and bake at 350° for 40 minutes.

Recipes from Iowa with Love...

Sioux City, located in the middle of one of the great hog-raising and cattle-feeding areas of the country, was the second largest meat-packing city in the early 1900's. It is a major food center, with honey-packing and popcorn plants in addition to the meat industry.

Steak and Bacon Roll-Ups

Serves 4

1 flank steak, 1-1½ pounds
1 teaspoon meat tenderizer
   (optional)
½ pound bacon
1 teaspoon garlic salt
½ teaspoon pepper
2 tablespoons chopped
   parsley
1 1½-ounce envelope
   hollandaise sauce mix
¼ teaspoon crushed
   tarragon

Have the butcher tenderize the flank steak, or apply meat tenderizer and pound until steak is ½" thick. Fry bacon until cooked but not crisp. Sprinkle steak with garlic salt and pepper. Score steak diagonally, making diamond-shaped cuts. Place bacon on the meat lengthwise and sprinkle with parsley. Roll steak up, starting at narrow end, and skewer with wooden picks at 1" intervals. Cut meat in 1" slices with electric knife. Grill over medium coals, or broil in oven for 10-15 minutes. Prepare hollandaise sauce according to package directions, adding tarragon to dry mix.

Recipes from Iowa with Love...

Every September, Fort Madison hosts the largest three-day rodeo in the Midwest. Beer and chili, or any variation of traditional Mexican food, is served for the occasion. The following treat is prepared by one local resident to serve his favorite cowpersons.

Father Jerry's Rodeo Enchiladas

Serves 4

½ large onion, chopped
2 cloves garlic, crushed
2 tablespoons oil
½ 4-ounce can green chilis, diced and seeded
1 1-pound can peeled tomatoes, or 6 fresh tomatoes, peeled and chopped
1 cup tomato juice
¼ teaspoon oregano
½ teaspoon basil
1½ tablespoons cornstarch

Saute onion and garlic in hot oil until onion is translucent. Add chilis, tomatoes, tomato juice and herbs. Simmer uncovered 20 minutes. Mix cornstarch in a little water and stir into sauce. Simmer another 10 minutes until thickened.

8 flour tortillas
10 ounces sharp Cheddar cheese, grated
2 tablespoons chopped parsley
2 or 3 green onions, chopped

Grease a 9×13" baking dish. Place 1 tortilla at a time on top of sauce until warm. Carefully remove to a plate with the sauce-covered side up. Arrange cheese, parsley and onions on tortilla and roll up. Place seam-side down in the baking dish. Spoon sauce over rolled tortillas and bake at 350° for 20 minutes. Additional shredded cheese and chopped ripe olives may be sprinkled on top before baking if desired.

Recipes from Iowa with Love...

Herbert Hoover, from West Branch, was the first United States president born west of the Mississippi River. He became the scapegoat for many of the problems of the Great Depression. Will Rogers once said, "I always did want to see Herbert Hoover elected. I wanted to see how far a competent man could go in politics. It has never been tried before."

Sour Cream Meatballs

"this recipe is so good...try it!"

Serves 6-8

2 **pounds ground beef**
1 **8-ounce carton**
   sour cream
1 **1½-ounce envelope**
   onion soup mix
1½ **cups bread crumbs**
1 **egg, slightly beaten**
⅓ **cup flour**
1 **teaspoon paprika**
¼ **cup butter**
1 **can cream of chicken**
   soup
¾ **cup milk**
   Noodles or rice

Mix ground beef, sour cream, onion soup mix, bread crumbs and egg together in large bowl. Form mixture into balls and roll in flour mixed with paprika. Heat butter in large skillet, and brown meatballs. Blend soup and milk together and pour over browned meatballs. Cover and simmer for 20 minutes. Serve over noodles or rice.

Recipes from Iowa with Love...

"Buffalo Bill" Cody was born near Le Claire and grew up to be an Indian scout, a buffalo hunter, a pony express rider, a hotel operator and a jack-of-all trades. When his friend Ned Buntline, the author, popularized him in western stories, he went on to become a hero of the West.

Pepper Steak

Serves 4

4 pounds boneless
   round steak
½ cup soy sauce
1 teaspoon garlic salt
2 cups beef broth
½ teaspoon ginger
1 cup boiling water
3 tablespoons oil
1½ cups water
3-4 large green peppers,
   cut into strips
2 medium onions, chopped
¼ cup cold water
6 tablespoons cornstarch
   Rice, brown rice or
   Chinese noodles

Trim fat, and cut meat into cubes. Combine soy sauce, garlic salt, beef broth, ginger and boiling water. Add beef and refrigerate for several hours. About 1½ hours before serving, drain meat, saving 2 cups marinade. Heat oil in a large skillet, add meat and brown quickly. Add reserved marinade, and 1½ cups water. Reduce heat, cover and simmer for 1 hour. Add peppers and onions and cook 15 minutes. Combine ¼ cup water with cornstarch and stir into hot pan liquid. Cook, stirring until mixture thickens. Serve over rice or Chinese noodles.

Recipes from Iowa with Love...

The rugged beauty of the wooded hills and spring-fed streams of northeast Iowa brought a large number of Norwegian immigrants to the Decorah area. The Norse specialty foods, crafts, folk dancing and music of the Decorah Nordic Fest each July makes this one of the most interesting events in Iowa.

Benlase Fugles (Birds)
"a Norwegian specialty"

Serves 6-8

3 pounds round steak,
    cut thin
½ pound bacon
1 teaspoon salt
½ teaspoon pepper
½ teaspoon cloves
⅛ teaspoon ginger
1 medium onion,
    chopped fine
2 tablespoons oil
1½ cups beef bouillon
1 apple, quartered
1 tablespoon flour

Trim fat from steak, pound on both sides, and cut into 2×3" pieces. Lay ½ strip of bacon on each piece of meat. Mix seasonings and onion together and sprinkle over meat strips. Roll meat and fasten with wooden picks. Brown in oil in a heavy pan. Drain excess oil, add bouillon and the apple and simmer 1 hour, or until tender. Remove meat and discard apple; add flour to pan broth and stir until smooth. Cook until thickened. Add meat to gravy to warm and serve over rice, noodles or potatoes.

Recipes from Iowa with Love...

Drawn by reports of rich soil and cheap land, immigrants poured into Iowa throughout the nineteenth century. An ad in an Eastern newspaper reported, "Taking into consideration the soil, the timber, the water, and the climate, the Iowa territory may be considered the best part of the Mississippi Valley." More of these immigrants were German than any other nationality.

Gefullte Nudeln
"German Filled Noodles with Beef Filling"

Serves 4

Filling
2 cups bread cubes
1 pound ground beef
½ cup finely chopped onion
2 eggs
1 teaspoon salt
⅛ teaspoon pepper
¼ teaspoon nutmeg

Noodles
2 eggs
½ cup water
1 teaspoon salt
1½ cups flour

Topping
1 cup finely rolled cracker crumbs
2 tablespoons butter

Soak bread cubes in water and press out excess water. Brown beef and onion over medium heat until beef is browned. Remove from heat and stir in bread cubes and remaining filling ingredients.

Beat eggs and water together. Add salt and flour and mix well. Knead dough slightly, adding more flour if needed. Roll out into two rectangles, 10×15". Put half the filling on half of each rectangle. Moisten edges of each with water. Fold unfilled portion over filled half and seal edges. With edge of hand, mark into 3×3" pieces, pressing firmly to seal. Cut along where you have pressed and check to make sure each noodle is sealed. In large kettle, bring 3 quarts water and 2 tablespoons salt to a boil. Drop in noodles and boil for 12-15 minutes. Remove with a slotted spoon to serving platter. Top with cracker crumbs that have been browned in butter. Delicious served with applesauce.

Recipes from Iowa with Love...

Terrace Hill, built in 1869, has been referred to as the greatest example of Victorian architecture between Chicago and California. It was the home of the Hubbell family for 87 years, and was given to the State of Iowa in 1971 by the Hubbell heirs. In 1972, the Iowa legislature enacted a bill designating Terrace Hill as the Iowa governor's mansion.

Tournedos Iowa

"this recipe is from Mrs. Robert Ray, First Lady of Iowa from 1969-1982"

Serves 4

2 tablespoons butter
½ cup sliced mushrooms
1 tablespoon flour
½ cup mushroom juice
¼ cup red wine
¼ teaspoon Worcestershire sauce
¼ teaspoon salt
Dash pepper
4 filets mignon
1 large ripe tomato

Melt butter and saute mushrooms in a small saucepan. Add flour and cook slowly a few minutes, until slightly browned. Stir in mushroom juice, wine, and seasonings. Cook until thickened. While this sauce is cooking, season and grill filets to taste. Cut the tomato into four slices and grill. Arrange tomato slice on each filet and pour mushroom sauce over all.

TERRACE HILL, DES MOINES, IOWA

The truckers who roar through Iowa on Interstates 35 and 80 chat to each other on their CB radios about "the Cornpatch", their name for Iowa.

Cornpatch Casserole
"tasty, inexpensive and easy to prepare ahead of time"

Serves 6-8

1 **green pepper, chopped**
1 **medium onion, chopped**
1 **tablespoon butter or oil**
1 **pound ground beef**
2 **cups shell macaroni**
1 **3½-ounce can mush-
   rooms, drained**
2 **8-ounce cans tomato
   sauce**
1 **17-ounce can cream-
   style corn**
½ **teaspoon celery salt
   Salt and pepper to taste**
¾ **cup sharp Cheddar
   cheese, grated**

Saute green pepper and onion in butter or oil. Add ground beef and brown lightly. Cook macaroni according to directions, drain, and add to meat. Add the remaining ingredients, except for cheese, mix well, and put in an oiled casserole. Sprinkle cheese over the top and bake at 300° for 45 minutes.

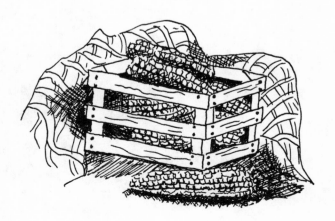

Recipes from Iowa with Love...

The first stage line into the Des Moines area was established in 1849, and connected Fort Des Moines to Keokuk. The local newspaper stated that the wagons arrived "with great regularity semi-occasionally."

Braised Beef Short Ribs

Serves 6-7

½ **cup chopped onion**
½ **cup chopped celery**
3 **tablespoons oil**
4 **tablespoons flour**
2 **teaspoons salt**
⅛ **teaspoon pepper**
¼ **teaspoon rosemary**
3 **pounds short ribs**
1½ **cups beef stock or condensed beef broth**
¼ **cup sherry (optional)**

Saute onion and celery in oil until glossy. Transfer vegetables to a large kettle with lid. Combine flour, salt, pepper and rosemary. Dredge ribs with seasoned flour; save remaining flour. Brown ribs in same oil used for vegetables. Transfer to kettle, add beef broth and cover. Bake at 350° for 2½ hours. Skim off excess fat. Mix remainder of seasoned flour with a little cold water and add to meat broth to thicken. Add ¼ cup sherry if desired. Combine gravy and ribs and simmer for 10 minutes. Serve with buttered baby carrots, tiny parsleyed potatoes, and broiled tomato halves.

Recipes from Iowa with Love...

Iowa's pioneers had to find their own remedies for illness and ailments. In his *"Circle of Useful Knowledge"* published in 1877, Charles Kinsley prescribed the following for a headache:

"Gather sumac leaves in the summer and dry in the sun until they can be crumbled into dust. Twice a day smoke the sumac leaves in a new pipe, and after two months, the headache should disappear."

No Headache Hamburger Noodle Casserole
"a good recipe for casual entertaining"

Serves 6

4 cups cooked noodles
1 tablespoon butter
1 cup cottage cheese
1 8-ounce package cream cheese
¼ cup sour cream
½ teaspoon salt
¼ teaspoon pepper
½ cup chopped onion
2 tablespoons green pepper
2 tablespoons butter
1 pound ground chuck
2 8-ounce cans tomato sauce
¾ cup grated sharp cheese

Place drained noodles in 2-quart casserole and mix in 1 tablespoon of butter. Mix cottage cheese, cream cheese, sour cream, salt and pepper till smooth and spread evenly over noodles. Saute onion and green pepper in 2 tablespoons butter till glossy; add meat and brown slightly. Add tomato sauce to meat mixture, and pour over top of layered ingredients in casserole. Sprinkle grated cheese on top and bake at 350° for 35 minutes.

Recipes from Iowa with Love...

The Ledges State Park was one of the first of our state parks. The sandstone cliffs, ledges and the nature trails add scenic appeal, while the Indian Council Ledge and the Indian mounds just south of the park add historical interest to this beautiful retreat.

Ledges Combination Rice Casserole

"sausage, beef, rice and mushrooms...excellent casserole"

Serves 12

1 **pound bulk sausage**
1 **pound ground beef**
1 **cup chopped celery**
1 **cup chopped onion**
1¼ **cups raw rice; white, brown or wild rice mix**
1 **3-ounce envelope chicken noodle soup mix**
5 **cups water**
1 **teaspoon salt**
2 **6-ounce cans mushrooms**
½ **cup chopped slivered almonds**
2 **cans cream of mushroom soup**
Juice of 1 lemon

Brown sausage, beef, celery and onion in large skillet until slightly browned. Drain. Add rice, soup mix, water, salt, mushrooms and almonds. Transfer ingredients to a large casserole (3-quart). Bake covered at 300° for 1½ hours. Add more water if necessary. Spread mushroom soup mixed with lemon juice over top of casserole and bake uncovered 20 minutes more.

Recipes from Iowa with Love...

The opening of the Des Moines Civic Center in 1979 was a significant step in the revitalization of downtown Des Moines. Nollen Plaza has become a focal point for activities appealing to all ages and interests, and the Crusoe Umbrella by Claes Oldenburg has become a symbol, not only of the Civic Center, but of a vigorous downtown.

Uptown Brisket

"a wonderful, easy recipe for entertaining"

Serves 8

4 **pounds brisket of beef**
¼ **cup liquid smoke**
1 **teaspoon onion salt**
1 **teaspoon garlic salt**
1 **teaspoon celery salt**
1½ **teaspoons Worcester-
    shire sauce**

Place brisket on heavy duty foil large enough to enclose meat. Put in a shallow baking dish. Mix remaining ingredients, brush over entire surface of the brisket, and seal in the foil. Refrigerate for 24 hours. Bake in foil at 275° for 5-5½ hours. Allow to rest for 20 minutes before slicing across the grain.

Recipes from Iowa with Love...

Iowa ranks third in the nation in the production of cattle, but the flavor of corn-fed Iowa beef is second to none.

Cold Sliced Brisket with Herb Mayonnaise

"wonderful for supper on a hot summer day"

Serves 6

4-5 pounds lean brisket
6 sprigs parsley
4 cloves peeled garlic, chopped
2 cups chopped celery, with leaves
1 large onion

2 bay leaves
4 cloves
½ teaspoon thyme
Salt and pepper to taste
Water to cover

Place all ingredients in a roaster. Simmer on top of the stove for 1 hour, skimming the top as necessary. Place in oven and bake at 275° for 3 hours. Remove brisket and allow to cool before slicing. (Broth should be reserved for soup or cooking.) Spoon Herb Mayonnaise over slices. Garnish with parsley.

Herb Mayonnaise

1 hard-cooked egg, sieved
1 egg yolk
4 tablespoons finely chopped onion
1 tablespoon Dijon mustard
1 tablespoon white vinegar
1 tablespoon chopped parsley
1 cup oil
1 teaspoon dried tarragon

1 tablespoon chopped chives
1 tablespoon lemon juice
3 drops red pepper sauce
½ teaspoon Worcestershire sauce
¾ teaspoon salt
Fresh-ground pepper
1 tablespoon cold water

Using a wire whisk, stir the sieved egg, egg yolk, onion, mustard, vinegar and parsley until blended. Beat oil in gradually till mixed; then beat vigorously until mixture is the consistency of mayonnaise. Stir in rest of ingredients.

Recipes from Iowa with Love...

New ways blend with old traditions in the Amana Colonies. The latest microwave equipment may be used to prepare the traditional German food that is served in their many fine restaurants. The annual Oktoberfest celebration honors the German heritage of most of the people of the Colonies.

Stuffed Cabbage Crown

"a family favorite from the Amana Colonies"

Serves 4

1 **pound ground beef**
⅓ **cup flour**
1½ **teaspoons salt**
¼ **teaspoon pepper**
1 **egg**
1 **cup milk**
1 **small onion, grated**
1 **head cabbage (3 pounds)**
1 **envelope dry onion soup mix**
1 **8-ounce package noodles**

Mix all the ingredients except cabbage, soup mix, and noodles with electric mixer until well blended. Set aside. Trim off outside leaves of cabbage and cut a slice 1" thick from core end and save. Cut core from cabbage and hollow out the head of cabbage with a sharp knife to make a shell ½" thick. Spoon meat mixture into shell. Fit cut slice back into place and tie securely with a string. Place stuffed cabbage, core end down, in large, heavy pan or dutch oven. Pour boiling water to almost cover and add onion soup mix. Cover and bake in 325° oven for 2½ hours. When done, lift cabbage head out and use broth to cook noodles for 8-10 minutes. Drain noodles and serve with the stuffed cabbage which has been cut in wedges.

Recipes from Iowa with Love...

The first National Hobo Convention was held in Britt, Iowa in 1900. Since 1933, the convention has become an annual event. This stew is served by the townspeople and is very tasty.

Hobo Mulligan Stew

"when you're expecting a crowd"

Serves 4,000

450	pounds stew meat
900	pounds of potatoes
250	pounds of carrots
35	pounds of green-red peppers
300	pounds cabbage
100	pounds turnips
150	pounds tomatoes
20	pounds salt
3	pounds chili pepper
12-	24 lbs rice
60	pounds celery
1	pound bay leaves
24	gallons of mixed vegetables
10	pounds kitchen bouquet flavoring

First, find a large kettle. Combine all ingredients except rice. Add enough water to make a total of 5,000 eight ounce cups. Simmer eight to nine hours. Add rice about ½-hour before serving.

Recipes from Iowa with Love...

Des Moines native Dan Hunter is a song writer, singer and humorist whose easy style and way with words are making a name for him nationwide.

Dan's Killer Chili

Serves 8-10

1 **Bermuda onion**
Many ribs of celery
Green pepper
1 **pound whole hog hot sausage**
1 **pound ground beef**
2 **teaspoons Worcestershire sauce**
Fresh ground pepper
Paprika
Chili powder

4 **fresh ripe tomatoes or 2 17-ounce cans tomatoes**
2 **small cans tomato paste**
1 **pound mushrooms**
Juice of 1 lemon
1 **bay leaf**
Oregano
Celery seed
Coriander

Killer Chili is not to be taken lightly; it can and should be made into a day-long project of preparation and feasting. Invite 8-10 friends and march the crew into the kitchen and begin slicing, dicing and paring the vegetables and whatever you can find. You are limited only by your imagination; if you have carrots, by all means slice them up. While your cronies are rattling sabers over the onions, celery, green pepper, you must begin to brown the meat in a big pan. While the meat is browning, add Worcestershire sauce, fresh ground pepper in vast quantities, paprika and chili powder. Have one of your associates open the canned goods and dump them with the mushrooms, lemon juice, and bay leaf into a cauldron or suitably sized pot and place over slow heat. When your friends have finished making little vegetables out of bigger vegetables, whisk the little devils into a frying pan and saute them until tender with a little juice from the browning meat. When

Dan's Killer Chili, Continued

the meat has succumbed to the low heat and has been browned into submission, dump the meat, juice and all, into the big pot, which should be simmering over low heat. Now comes the time to display your personal genius for alchemy. Do not concern yourself with ½ teaspoon of this or 1¼ tablespoons of that, just start grabbing spices and dump and sprinkle to your heart's content. Cook the whole concoction for 2-4 hours or until your mouth watering tongues can't wait any longer. Serve with bread, cheese and crackers. For an appetizer, why not have your guests run around the house a few times. You may wonder why there are no beans in this recipe. If you want beans, fine, dump them in if you're so inclined. A good test of Killer Chili is to drop a few beans into the bubbling cauldron; if they hop out running, the chili could be too hot. However, if the beans rise up slowly and casually walk away humming Mexican folk tunes, you have reached an acceptable degree and will be able to witness actual walkin' beans.

[Dan's well known folk song *Walkin' Beans* refers to going through the soybean fields to hoe weeds and volunteer corn from around the young plants.]

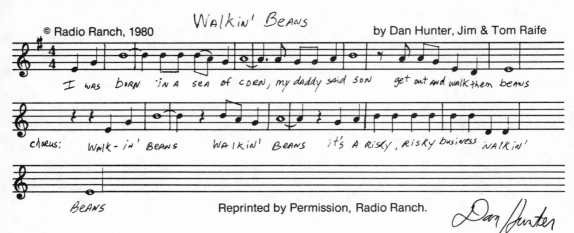

Walkin' Beans

© Radio Ranch, 1980   by Dan Hunter, Jim & Tom Raife

I was born in a sea of corn, my daddy said son   get out and walk them beans

chorus: Walk-in' Beans   Walkin' Beans   it's a risky, risky business walkin'

Beans   Reprinted by Permission, Radio Ranch.

Recipes from Iowa with Love...

Forest City is called the recreation vehicle capital of the world. Winnebago Industries has sold more than 125,000 units, from the small campers to the large motor homes. Each summer, the Grand National Rally in Forest City draws hundreds of Winnebago owners from all over the country.

Winnebago Burgers
"as served in Forest City"

Serves 6-8

2 **pounds ground chuck**
1 **teaspoon salt**
½ **teaspoon pepper**
⅛ **teaspoon garlic powder**

Mix ingredients together and grill over medium coals until done to your liking. Serve with the Burger Sauce and a large plate with lettuce, crisp fried bacon slices, chopped onions, tomato slices and cheese slices.

Burger Sauce
2 **tablespoons dry mustard**
2 **tablespoons water**
1 **cup ketchup**
½ **teaspoon Worcestershire sauce**

Mix ingredients together and let people ladle on amount they wish.

Tuna Crunch Casserole
"a good family casserole with an Oriental flavor"

Serves 4

- 1 6½-ounce can tuna
- 1 2½-ounce jar sliced mushrooms
- ½ cup sliced celery
- 2 tablespoons sliced green onions
- 1 6-ounce can mushroom soup
- 2 tablespoons water
- 2 teaspoons soy sauce
- ½ cup sliced water chestnuts
- 1 can chow mein noodles

Drain tuna and break into small chunks. Add mushrooms, celery and onions. Mix soup with water and soy sauce; add to tuna mixture. Add water chestnuts and ½ can noodles (reserve rest for topping.) Toss gently and put into small casserole. Sprinkle remaining noodles on top and bake at 375° for 30 minutes.

The first bridge spanning the Mississippi River was built in 1856 between Rock Island, Ill., and what is now downtown Davenport. Davenport and Bettendorf, together with Rock Island and Moline, Ill., make up the Quad Cities.

Pork Chops a' la McKee

"tender chops with a wonderful sauce"

Serves 4

4 **butterfly pork chops**
2 **tablespoons flour, seasoned with salt and pepper**
1 **tablespoon oil**
1 **lemon, sliced**
1 **medium onion, sliced**
1 **medium green pepper, sliced**
2 **cups tomato juice**

Make 3 small slashes around edge of each pork chop to keep from curling. Dust with seasoned flour and brown lightly in moderately hot oil. Place meat in baking dish. Arrange 1 slice each of lemon, onion and green pepper on each chop. Tuck any remaining slices around the sides. Pour tomato juice over the top, cover and bake at 325° for 1 hour.

Recipes from Iowa with Love...

Private Merle Hay of Glidden was one of the first three American soldiers killed in World War I. France erected a monument in his honor, and one of the major streets of Des Moines was named for him.

Hearty Hero

Serves 4

1   1-pound loaf unsliced Vienna bread
1½ pounds ground pork
1   medium onion, chopped
1   rib celery, chopped
2   cloves garlic, minced
½   cup barbecue sauce
1½ teaspoons chili powder
½   teaspoon salt
1   cup shredded Cheddar cheese

Cut a shallow slice 2" wide from top of bread. Hollow inside of loaf until sides are ½" thick. Brown pork, onion, celery and garlic in large skillet. Pour off drippings. Add barbecue sauce, chili powder and salt; mix. Line bottom of inside of loaf with ½ cup cheese. Add the meat mixture and sprinkle remaining cheese over meat. Place the top back on loaf. Wrap in foil, sealing top and ends. Place on a cookie sheet and bake at 450° for 20 minutes. Let stand 10 minutes before slicing.

Recipes from Iowa with Love...

The Iowa Chop is a thick cut, taken from the center portion of the pork loin. Whether it's baked, grilled or fried, it's an inch and a half of pure pleasure.

Grilled Iowa Chops

"add a few wet hickory chips to the coals for extra flavor"

Serves 6

6 Iowa chops, center cut
1¼ - 1½" thick
Salt and pepper to taste

Barbecue Sauce

½ **cup butter**
½ **cup ketchup**
2 **tablespoons vinegar**
1 **tablespoon lemon juice**
1 **tablespoon Dijon mustard**
1 **tablespoon Worcester-**
shire sauce
½ **teaspoon garlic powder**
2 **tablespoons firmly packed**
brown sugar

Place chops on grill 6" above medium coals. Grill for 20 minutes. Turn chops, baste with barbecue sauce. Continue to baste and turn as needed for another 20-30 minutes.

Melt butter, add rest of the ingredients and bring to a boil. Stir for 1 minute and remove from heat.

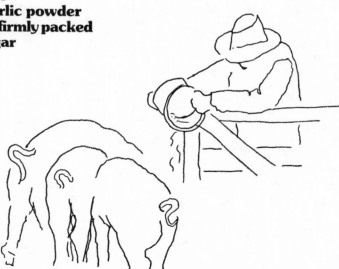

Recipes from Iowa with Love...

Who would know how to prepare pork chops better than the Iowa Pork Producers and their wives, the Porkettes! This recipe for Iowa chops comes from them, and it is delicious.

Cornbread Stuffed Chops
"treat your family to tenderness"

Serves 4

4 Iowa chops, 1¼ - 1½" thick
2 cups crumbled cornbread
¼ cup chopped onion
¼ cup chopped green pepper
¼ cup melted butter
1 beaten egg
**1 tablespoon chopped
       pimento (optional)**
½ teaspoon salt
⅛ teaspoon pepper

Savory Glaze
½ cup ketchup
2 tablespoons brown sugar
**2 teaspoons prepared
       mustard**
¼ teaspoon chili powder

Cut pocket in chops by cutting into the center from the rib side, parallel to the rib bone and the surface of the chop. In medium mixing bowl, toss together cornbread, onion, green pepper, butter, egg, pimento, salt and pepper. Fill pockets of chops, dividing stuffing evenly between chops. Arrange chops in a 2-quart shallow baking dish (12×8×2"). Prepare glaze by mixing ingredients together. Brush half of glaze over top of chops. Cover with foil. Bake in a 350° oven 1 hour, or until chops are tender. Brush with remaining glaze before serving.

The success of the Friendship Force indicates how much Iowans love to travel. Almost every traveler brings home stories of the couple from Algona they met in Venezuela or the group from Oskaloosa they met in Ireland.

French Cheese and Ham Crepes

"served to Iowans in Paris by their elegant French hostess"

Serves 6

Basic Crepe Recipe
- 2 **eggs**
- 2 **egg yolks**
- 1 **cup milk**
- 1 **cup flour**
- ¼ **teaspoon baking powder**
- ½ **teaspoon salt**
- 1 **tablespoon sugar**
- 3 **tablespoons oil**

Beat eggs and egg yolks slightly. Add milk. Sift flour, baking powder and salt together and stir into egg mixture. Add sugar and oil; beat until smooth. To cook, brush a crepe pan or a heavy, 6" skillet with butter and heat until moderately hot. Add 1 tablespoon batter to skillet, tip skillet until the thin batter covers the bottom. Cook quickly on both sides. Prepare 12 crepes. They may be cooked earlier, stacked using wax paper to separate, and reheated.

Ham and Cheese Filling
- 4 **tablespoons soft butter**
- 12 **thin slices ham**
- 4 **cups grated cheese, Mozzarella or Swiss Jarlsberg**

Spread soft butter on each cooked crepe. Place 1 slice of ham on each crepe, sprinkle ¼ cup cheese in a strip down the center of the crepe, fold in thirds toward the center. Sprinkle remaining cheese on top of the folded crepes. Bake at 350° for 10-12 minutes.

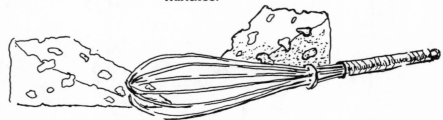

Recipes from Iowa with Love...

JoAnn Fangman had La Petite Ecole in Clear Lake, and deserves credit for much of the fine cooking found in that part of Iowa. After her death in a car accident, a group of her students put together the cookbook she had always planned to do, *"The Mousse and Me."* Our thanks to the Fangman family and those who wrote the book for letting us use this recipe from the book.

Filet De Porc Cauchoise

"superb"

1	tablespoon oil	3	shallots, chopped
2	tablespoons butter	1	clove garlic, crushed
3-4	pounds boned pork loin		Bouquet garni (bay leaf,
2	onions, chopped		parsley, peppercorns,
2	tablespoons flour		rosemary and marjoram)
1½	cups chicken stock		Salt and pepper
1	cup beef stock	2	teaspoons soy sauce
1	cup white wine		(optional)

Heat oil and butter, brown pork on all sides. Take out, add onions, cook until translucent. Add flour and cook, stirring until browned. At once, add 2 cups of the stock with wine, shallots, garlic, bouquet garni, and seasoning, and replace the pork. Cover and bake at 325° for 1½ hours or until meat is very tender, adding more stock if necessary. Take pork out, cut in thin diagonal slices and return to the sauce.

For the garnish:

¼	cup butter	1	pound whole mushrooms,
1	small head celery, about		stems trimmed
	4 cups, cut diagonally	½	cup English walnut halves
	in 1" chunks	1	teaspoon curry powder
	Salt and pepper	2	tablespoons minced parsley

Melt butter in saucepan, add celery with salt and pepper, press piece of waxed paper on top. Cover with lid and cook very gently until celery is just tender. Add the mushrooms and continue cooking, uncovered until tender. Add the walnuts and curry powder and mix carefully. Taste for seasoning. When ready to serve, arrange pork slices overlapping on one side of platter, skim any fat from sauce, taste for final seasoning, add soy sauce to taste, and spoon a little over the pork. Spoon garnish down other side of platter. Sprinkle with parsley, reheat remaining sauce and serve it separately.

The Iowa Machine Shed in Davenport won the Iowa Pork Producers Cookoff with this recipe for Stuffed Pork Loin. The Machine Shed specializes in food that is typically Iowan.

Stuffed Pork Loin

"the aristocrat of the pork roasts, dressed up a bit"

Serves 14-18

1½ **pounds dried bread cubes**
1 **quart chicken stock**
½ **pound butter, melted**
1 **small bunch celery, diced**
1 **white onion, diced**
7-9 **pound boneless pork loin**
Sage, garlic salt, salt and pepper to taste

Moisten bread cubes with chicken stock and add melted butter. Add celery and onion. Mix well. Cut the loin in half across width, then cut each half butterfly fashion, not clear through. Open loins fat side down and place half of the stuffing along the center of each. Roll up loin and tie with butcher string. Season with sage, garlic salt, salt and pepper. Roast at 325° for 2 to 3 hours. (Inside temperature must be 170°.) Mix drippings with flour to make gravy.

A restaurant honoring the Iowa farmer.

Recipes from Iowa with Love...

The first cookbook to give ingredient amounts by precise measurements was the *Boston Cooking-School Cook Book* published in 1896. Until then "receipts" would specify "butter as large as an egg" or "three hands full of flour". This may be the reason many of us remember that our grandmothers never measured when they cooked.

Fried Rice With Ham

"an easy and delicious way to use leftover ham"

Serves 4

1⅓ cups raw rice
1½ cups cooked ham
    in strips or cubes
 1 medium onion, chopped
½ cup chopped green
    pepper
½ cup sliced celery
 2 tablespoons oil
 1 teaspoon MSG
   Salt and pepper to taste
 2 tablespoons soy sauce
 2 eggs

Cook rice according to directions on package for firm texture; cool. Place ham, onion, green pepper, celery and oil in a large skillet; saute until vegetables are glossy. Add MSG, salt and pepper, mixing well. Add rice and soy sauce, and stir. Break eggs into the mixture and cook over medium heat, stirring constantly, until eggs are set.

Recipes from Iowa with Love...

One of the rites of summer for some Iowa teen-agers is detasseling corn. It gives them a chance to earn good money while they get a tan. Hybrid corn is detasseled to keep the seed line pure.

Ham and Corn Bake

Serves 6

3 tablespoons flour
3 tablespoons butter
1½ cups milk
1 teaspoon dry mustard
½ teaspoon Worcester-
    shire sauce
½ teaspoon salt
¼ teaspoon pepper
1 17-ounce can corn
1 medium onion, chopped
½ cup chopped green
    pepper
2 cups diced cooked ham
½ cup grated Cheddar
    cheese
Bread crumbs for
    topping

Cook flour and butter in saucepan. Gradually add milk to form a white sauce. Add seasonings, corn, onion, green pepper and ham. Transfer ingredients to a 2-quart casserole. Top with cheese and bread crumbs, and bake at 350° for 30 minutes.

Recipes from Iowa with Love...

"This little piggy went to market," and, in Iowa, a lot of others joined him. Iowa ranked number one in the nation in hog production in 1981, furnishing 28 percent of the total for the entire country.

Cheesy Pork Loaf

"this meatloaf is different and delicious"

Serves 4

1½ **pounds lean ground pork**
2 **slightly beaten eggs**
¼ **pound sharp cheese, cubed fine**
¾ **cup fine cracker crumbs**
⅓ **cup milk**
¼ **cup chopped onion**
½ **cup tomato sauce**

Thoroughly mix all ingredients except tomato sauce. Mold into a loaf and place in a shallow baking dish. Bake at 350° for 1½ hours. Drizzle tomato sauce on top during the last 30 minutes.

Recipes from Iowa with Love...

Iowa is called the "Hawkeye State" in honor of the great Sac and Fox Indian chief, Black Hawk. In one of his last speeches, at the celebration of Iowa's becoming a territory, Black Hawk said, "The earth is our mother; we are now on it with the Great Spirit above us. It is good...I loved my towns, my cornfields and the home of my people. I fought for it. It is now yours; keep it as we did; it will produce you good crops."

Fish Fillets in Wine Sauce

Serves 2

2 tablespoons butter
  Juice of 1 lemon
1 tablespoon dry mustard
3 ounces white wine
2 fish fillets, fresh or frozen
  Salt, pepper and paprika

Cook butter, lemon juice and mustard in small saucepan until mixture begins to brown. Add wine and simmer until sauce is reduced to ½ volume. Pour half the sauce into flat baking dish and add the fish. Sprinkle with salt, pepper and paprika. Cover with remaining sauce. Broil for 10 minutes. Cover dish with foil and bake at 400° for 20-25 minutes.

Heavenly Sole

Serves 4

2 **pounds sole fillets**
2 **tablespoons lemon juice**
½ **cup Parmesan cheese**
¼ **cup soft margarine**
3 **tablespoons mayonnaise**
3 **tablespoons chopped
    green onion**
   Dash salt

Place fillets in a single layer in a flat baking dish. Brush with lemon juice and let stand 10 minutes. Broil fillets 6-8 minutes or until fish flakes easily. Combine remaining ingredients and spread over fish. Broil 2-3 minutes or until lightly browned.

Recipes from Iowa with Love...

Streams, lakes and rivers provide opportunity for the Iowa fisherman. Iowa has 19,000 miles of interior rivers and streams. It also has the lakes of the northwest region, four of the nation's largest man-made lakes, and is bordered by the Mississippi and Missouri rivers.

Iowa Fish Chowder
"wonderful served with salad and bread"

Serves 6

⅓ cup flour
⅓ cup bacon fat or butter
1½ cups chopped onion
1 clove garlic, minced
⅔ cup chopped green
     pepper
2 cups tomato sauce
6 cups water
1 tablespoon Worcester-
     shire sauce
8 whole cloves
     dash of red pepper sauce
1 tablespoon paprika
1 bay leaf
1 teaspoon salt
¼ teaspoon pepper
1½ cups diced potatoes
1½ pounds fish fillets
     Thin lemon slices for
       garnish

Brown flour and bacon drippings or butter lightly. Add onion, garlic and green pepper; cook 5 minutes. Add remaining ingredients, except for fish and lemon; simmer, covered, for 30 minutes.

Cut fish into 1-inch pieces. Add to mixture and simmer, covered, 10-15 minutes. Float lemon slices on top when serving.

Recipes from Iowa with Love...

Burlington was called Catfish Bend by the early settlers. One settler paid $50 for the privilege of renaming the village for his home town of Burlington, Vermont. In 1838, it became the first capital of Iowa.

Riverboat Fried Catfish

"one of the ways catfish is prepared in the river towns"

Serves 4

2 **tablespoons bacon fat**
3 **tablespoons oil**
3 **tablespoons butter**
½ **cup crushed wheat flakes**
6 **tablespoons flour**
1 **teaspoon salt**
⅛ **teaspoon pepper**
1 **egg, slightly beaten**
1 **tablespoon water**
4 **catfish**

Heat bacon fat, oil and butter in a large skillet. Combine crushed wheat flakes, flour, salt and pepper. Mix egg and water. Dip fish into egg, then flour mixture. Place in hot fat, which should be deep enough to reach the center of the backbone of the fish as it lays on its side. Fry at 360° until golden brown on both sides.

Parker's Lamb Stew

Serves 12

3 tablespoons oil
3 pounds lamb shoulder,
    cut in 2" cubes
2 onions, sliced
2 garlic cloves, minced
1 cup chopped celery
¼ cup chopped parsley
2½ cups canned tomatoes
1 bay leaf, crumbled
½ teaspoon thyme
1 teaspoon salt
    Freshly ground pepper
2½ cups water
12 small carrots
6 potatoes, quartered
1 cup peas, frozen
½ cup flour
¾ cup cold water

Heat oil in a large, heavy kettle. Add lamb and brown. Add onions, garlic, celery, parsley, tomatoes, bay leaf, thyme, salt, pepper and 2½ cups water. Bring to a boil, reduce heat, cover and simmer 2 hours. Add carrots and potatoes, cover, and simmer 45 minutes. Add peas, cook 5 minutes. Blend flour with cold water and stir into stew. Simmer for 5 minutes.

Recipes from Iowa with Love...

Polo and cricket matches were favorite ways of spending leisure time in part of Northwest Iowa in the 1880's. The Close brothers, Cambridge graduates and land developers, bought huge tracts of land near LeMars and sold farms to Englishmen with enough capital to become stock farmers. This recipe comes from Bev Brodie, whose ancestors were among the settlers from England, and who is now "Country Cooking" columnist of the LeMars Daily Sentinel and editor of three cookbooks by that name.

Roast Leg of Lamb

Serves 8-10

Leg of lamb (6½-7 pounds)
1 large garlic clove, peeled and cut lengthwise into 8 thin slices
1 teaspoon oregano
1 teaspoon salt
¼ teaspoon freshly ground pepper
6 tablespoons lemon juice

Make ¼" incisions in 8 places on the fat side of the lamb and insert a sliver of garlic in each. Combine oregano, salt and pepper; press the mixture firmly all over the surface of the lamb. Place lamb, fat side up, on a rack in a shallow roasting pan. The lamb should roast at 325° for 30-35 minutes per pound, or until a meat thermometer registers 170-175°. Baste with lemon juice every 20 minutes.

Veal Scaloppine with Mushrooms

Serves 4

1 pound veal, thinly sliced
¼ cup flour
6 tablespoons butter
8 large mushroom caps
1 clove garlic, minced
¾ cup canned bouillon
¼ cup dry white wine
1 teaspoon cornstarch
Salt and pepper to taste

Pound veal lightly with meat mallet. Dredge in flour. Heat butter in skillet and brown veal on both sides. Remove to a warm plate. Saute mushrooms for 2 or 3 minutes. Add minced garlic, bouillon, wine and cornstarch, and let simmer for 5 minutes. Return veal to hot mixture, heat thoroughly and season with salt and pepper, if needed.

Recipes from Iowa with Love...

When asking people for recipes, we found they often began by offering recipes for entertaining. Then they would mention they had one the family asked for again and again, but "it was kind of different." This is one of those recipes that has been loved by four generations.

True's Sandwich
"really a meal"

Serves 1

3 **slices white or whole wheat toast**
6 **slices bacon, cooked crisp**
3 **slices ripe tomato (more if small)**
1½ **or more slices raw onion, according to taste**
   Salt and pepper

Stack each slice of toast with 2 slices bacon, 1 large slice tomato and ½ slice raw onion. Salt and pepper vegetables lightly if desired. Stack together toast slices and their toppings. Use wooden picks to hold shape. Cover with Hot Bacon Gravy and serve as a full meal with a knife and a fork.

Hot Bacon Gravy
3 **tablespoons flour**
3 **tablespoons bacon grease**
1 **cup warm milk**
½ **teaspoon salt**
¼ **teaspoon pepper**

Add flour to hot bacon grease and stir constantly for 2 minutes, or until mixture begins to bubble. Remove pan from heat and add warm milk gradually, stirring constantly. Add salt and pepper. Return pan to heat and stir until gravy thickens.

Recipes from Iowa with Love...

The Mississippi River, Iowa's eastern border, and the Missouri River on our west are major flyways, which makes Iowa a haven for birds of many types. Forney's Lake in southwest Iowa is a shallow marsh where as many as 300,000 waterfowl have been counted as they stop to feed and rest during their annual migration pattern.

Sauerkraut-Stuffed Wild Goose

"as prepared by a Des Moines sportsman and fine cook"

Serves 10

1 10-pound goose
1 large onion, chopped
1 tablespoon butter
6½ cups drained sauerkraut
1½ cups grated raw potato
1 medium apple, pared and diced
2 teaspoons caraway seed
½ teaspoon salt
¼ teaspoon pepper
½ cup Rhine wine

Prepare goose for stuffing. Saute onion in butter until golden brown. Add remaining ingredients, and cook for 5 minutes over medium heat, stirring constantly. Fill the cavity of the goose with the stuffing. Tuck legs under band of skin or tie to tail; twist wing tips under back. Place breast side up on a rack in a shallow roasting pan. Roast at 325° for about 4 hours.

Recipes from Iowa with Love...

Iowa is one of the top pheasant states in the country. These beautiful game birds are found in every section of the state. The Iowa Conservation Commission carefully controls the hunting season, and in 1981 nearly 1,500,000 were harvested by hunters.

Bob's Pheasant in Wine Sauce

Serves 6

1 cup flour
½ teaspoon salt
¼ teaspoon pepper
2 pheasants, cut in pieces
2 tablespoons oil
1 can cream of mushroom soup
½ cup white wine
½ cup water
1 bay leaf
1 large onion, sliced
⅔ cup melted butter
1 tablespoon straight bourbon

Mix flour, salt and pepper in paper sack. Drop pheasant pieces into sack and shake to lightly coat each piece. Heat oil in heavy skillet and brown on all sides. Set aside. Mix soup, wine, water and bay leaf; pour into large casserole. Put pheasant into casserole and spread sliced onion on top. Pour melted butter over all; cover and bake at 350° 1 hour or until tender. Shortly before serving, add bourbon to sauce. Remove pheasant to warm platter and pour sauce over the top.

Vegetables
and
Side Dishes

Spinach and Spaghetti

Serves 8

- **2 10-ounce packages frozen chopped spinach**
- **1½ pounds Monterey Jack cheese, shredded**
- **2 eggs, beaten**
- **1 cup sour cream**
- **2 tablespoons minced onion**
- **1 8-ounce package spaghetti, cooked**

Thaw spinach, squeeze juice out with hands. Shred cheese, reserving 1 cup for topping, and mix with eggs and sour cream. Add spinach, onion and cooked spaghetti. Mix. Pour into a 9×13″ oiled baking dish, and sprinkle reserved cheese on top. Bake at 350° for 30 minutes.

Recipes from Iowa with Love...

Iowa is indeed "where the tall corn grows." Iowa consistently leads the nation in the production of corn and furnishes around 20 percent of the total for the country. The tallest corn stalk on record is 31 feet 3 inches and was grown in Washington, Iowa.

Frozen Sweet Corn

"freeze it at the peak of the season"

8   cups corn, cut off the cob
1   teaspoon salt
2   tablespoons sugar
1   cup margarine
½   cup water

Bring all ingredients to a boil. Remove from heat, cool and freeze. Corn will be ready to eat as soon as thoroughly heated after being frozen.

Frozen Creamed Sweet Corn

8   cups corn, cut off the cob
1   teaspoon salt
1   tablespoon sugar
1   cup butter or margarine
1   pint light cream

Put the corn in a 9×13" oiled baking dish. Mix remaining ingredients together and pour over corn. Bake at 350° for 1 hour. Cool and freeze.

Skillet Sweet Corn

"cream corn right off the cob"

Serves 4

6 ears corn
6 tablespoons butter
½ cup light cream
½ teaspoon salt
½ teaspoon sugar
Ground pepper to taste

Husk corn and remove silks. Slice off kernels with a long, sharp knife or electric knife. Using back of a dinner knife, scrape milky substance from cob into the corn. Heat butter in skillet, add corn and milky substance, cook and stir 3-4 minutes. Add cream and seasonings. Stir over low heat for 2-3 minutes.

Best Way to Remove Silk from Corn Ears

"found in a Josef Mossman column"

Wad two paper towels into a ball. Leave both the corn and towels dry. Rub up and down on the corn briskly with the towels, turning the ear as you rub. This is faster than using a brush.

When Serving Corn to a Crowd

"will hold corn for several hours"

Boil corn-on-the cob as you usually do, being careful not to overcook. Cover corn with milk and hold at a warm temperature, but do not allow to boil. Float several tablespoons of butter on top of milk.

Corn was one of the first foods planted by the frontier settlers. It grew and stored well, so the early farm women were always looking for new and tasty ways to prepare it.

Cornmeal Polenta with Cheese

Serves 8

1 cup corn meal
1 teaspoon salt
1 cup cold water
3 cups boiling water
2 tablespoons butter
4 tablespoons grated
    Parmesan cheese
4 tablespoons oil
1 large onion, thinly sliced
1 cup thinly sliced fresh
    mushrooms
1 large clove garlic, minced
1 20-ounce can Italian
    tomatoes, chopped
1 6-ounce can tomato paste
2 tablespoons minced
    parsley
  Salt and pepper to taste
¼ pound Mozzarella cheese,
    sliced thin

Mix corn meal with salt and cold water. Add mixture slowly to boiling water, stirring constantly. Simmer 20 minutes on low heat, stirring frequently. Stir in butter and 2 tablespoons of Parmesan cheese. Pour into greased shallow pan and chill at least 4 hours. Pour 2 tablespoons oil into heavy saucepan, add onion, mushrooms, and garlic. Saute until onion is tender; add tomatoes and tomato paste and simmer 10 minutes. Add parsley and salt and pepper to taste. Cut chilled polenta into ½″ slices. Put 1 layer of slices in an oiled 9×13″ baking dish. Top with Mozzarella cheese and pour ½ the sauce over cheese. Make another layer with remaining polenta slices, pour remaining sauce over them and sprinkle with remaining Parmesan cheese that has been mixed with remaining oil. Bake at 350° for 30 minutes.

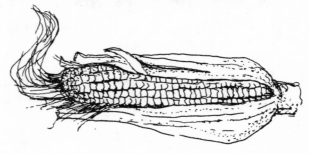

Recipes from Iowa with Love...

When you spot a bumper sticker or a button that says "Bix lives," you know you've found a lover of jazz. Bix Beiderbecke of Davenport has been called "the greatest hot jazz player of them all." He died in 1931 at the age of 28, and in 1971, the Bix Beiderbecke Festival was organized. Each summer, thousands bring their blankets to sit on the Mississippi levee in Davenport and listen to two days of fine jazz by bands from every part of the country.

Jazzy Green Beans
"with corn-on the cob and crusty bread, you have a meal"

Serves 4

1 pound fresh green beans, washed and snapped in bite-size pieces
1 12-ounce package smoke-flavored link sausages

Put beans in a large kettle. Cut sausages into bite-size pieces and add to beans. Cover with water, bring to a boil, turn heat to simmer, and cook covered until beans are fork-tender. Do not overcook. This can be done early in the day, refrigerated after cooling and reheated when ready to serve. This allows the flavors to blend.

Recipes from Iowa with Love...

When college football scholarships covered only tuition and books, even star athletes had to pay most of their college expenses. Duke Slater, all-American tackle on the University of Iowa football team of 1921, earned his meals by peeling potatoes. He graduated from law school and, in later years, became one of the few Blacks appointed as a circuit judge in Chicago.

Potato Pancakes with Applesauce

"simple to make with frozen hashbrowns"

Serves 4

1 12-ounce package frozen shredded hashbrown potatoes
2 eggs, beaten
1 tablespoon flour
2 tablespoons milk
¼ teaspoon salt
1 tablespoon minced onion
¼ cup shortening
Applesauce

Thaw potatoes. Mix eggs, flour, milk, salt and onion. Add to potatoes and mix. Heat shortening in a heavy skillet. Drop a heaping tablespoon of potato mixture into hot shortening and flatten with the spoon. Repeat for each cake. Cook until golden brown on bottom, turn and brown other side. Edges will be crisp and lacy. The pancakes are delicious served with applesauce.

Recipes from Iowa with Love...

A Taste of Terrace Hill is a collection of pictures, stories and recipes from the home that is now the Iowa governor's mansion, from the time it was built until present. It is published by the Terrace Hill Society and dedicated to the mansion's restoration and preservation.

Buffet Potato Casserole
"from a *Taste of Terrace Hill*"

Serves 12

1 2-pound package frozen hash brown potatoes
½ cup butter or margarine, melted
1 pint sour cream
1 can condensed cream of chicken soup
½ cup chopped onion
2 cups shredded Cheddar cheese
1 teaspoon salt
½ teaspoon pepper
2 cups corn flake crumbs
½ cup butter or margarine, melted

Combine potatoes and ½ cup melted butter in large bowl. Stir in sour cream, soup, onion, cheese, salt and pepper. Place in greased 13×9×2" baking dish. Combine corn flake crumbs and ½ cup melted butter. Sprinkle over top. Cover with foil. Bake in 350° oven 20 minutes. Uncover and continue baking 20 minutes.

Note: The casserole can be made in advance and refrigerated. If so, add 10 minutes to baking time.

Recipes from Iowa with Love...

Survival for an Iowa pioneer family depended on their ability to preserve food for use during the winter months. Onions were braided by their tops and hung where they would be dry, but not freeze. They would keep most of the winter.

Onion Pie

Serves 6

1 cup saltine crackers, finely crushed
½ cup melted butter
2 cups thinly sliced onions
2 tablespoons butter
⅔ cup milk
2 slightly beaten eggs
½ cup shredded sharp Cheddar cheese

Combine crackers and melted butter; mix well. Press into 8-inch pie plate to form crust. Saute onions in 2 tablespoons butter over medium heat until glossy. Put into cracker crust. Mix milk, eggs and cheese; pour over onions. Bake at 350° for 30 minutes.

Broccoli-Cauliflower Supreme

"a beautiful presentation"

Serves 6

1 **bunch fresh broccoli**
1 **medium head cauliflower**
6 **slices bacon, chopped**
¼ **cup chopped onion**
3 **tablespoons brown sugar**
3 **tablespoons vinegar**
1 **teaspoon salt**
¼ **teaspoon pepper**

Remove stems and cut broccoli flowerets; cook in boiling, salted water until tender but still crisp. Drain thoroughly. Cut as much of stem from cauliflower as possible while still keeping head intact. Cook in boiling, salted water until tender but still crisp. Drain thoroughly. Fry bacon until crisp, remove and drain. Using 3 tablespoons of bacon drippings, cook onion until soft. Stir in remaining ingredients and simmer for 3 minutes. To serve, place cauliflower head in center of serving plate and arrange broccoli in a ring around it. This can be assembled and left at room temperature for up to 2 hours. It is not necessary for it to be hot. Pour the hot sauce over vegetables and add crumbled bacon just before serving.

Slick-Trick Broccoli Sauté

"cook it briefly early in the day and warm it at serving time"

Serves 6

1½ **to 2 pounds fresh broccoli**
2 **quarts water, salted**
4 **tablespoons butter**
¼ **cup snipped parsley**

Wash broccoli and separate into stem pieces and flowerets. Trim and peel stem pieces, cut into 1″ chunks. Drop into boiling water; cook 2 minutes. Add flowerets and cook for another 2 minutes. Drain well in colander. Plunge into cold water till cool. Drain and chill till serving time. Melt butter in large skillet. Add broccoli; cook, shaking pan frequently, until heated through. Toss with parsley.

Corn and Broccoli Scallop

Serves 6-8

2   10-ounce packages frozen
     chopped broccoli
1   16½-ounce can cream
     style corn
½   cup cracker crumbs
1   egg, beaten
1   tablespoon minced onion
     Salt and pepper
1   tablespoon butter
1   cup grated Cheddar
     cheese

Thaw broccoli and drain very well. Place in a greased 2-quart casserole. Mix corn, cracker crumbs, egg, onion, salt and pepper and pour over broccoli. Dot with butter and sprinkle with grated cheese. Bake at 350° for 45 minutes.

Cheese Strata
"like a souffle"

Serves 4

5 slices stale bread,
   buttered
¾ cup shredded sharp
   Cheddar cheese
4 eggs, beaten
1 teaspoon dry mustard
2 cups milk
½ teaspoon salt
¼ teaspoon white pepper

Break or cut bread into pieces and put half into a well-greased 2-quart casserole. Add half the cheese, remaining bread, and the rest of the cheese. Put eggs and mustard into a bowl, mix. Add milk, salt and pepper; pour over the cheese and bread. Allow to stand several hours or overnight. Bake at 350° for 1-1½ hours.

Iowa is the fourth largest cheese-producing state in the country. Newton, Kalona, and the "Little Switzerland" area in northeast Iowa all have thriving cheese industries.

Cheese Peta
"a traditional Serbian dish"

Serves 8

¾ **pound cheese; Cheddar, American, Mozzarella**
½ **cup butter**
3 **heaping tablespoons flour**
2 **pounds cottage cheese, drained**
6 **eggs, beaten slightly**

Cut assorted cheeses and butter into ½" cubes and place in large bowl. Mix flour into cottage cheese and add to cheeses and butter. Add eggs and mix well. Pour into 2-quart casserole or 2 (9") pie pans and bake at 350° for 1 hour.

Recipes from Iowa with Love...

The second Fort Des Moines was built at the fork of the Raccoon and Des Moines rivers in 1843. The primary reason it was built was to keep aggressive whites from claiming land not open for development. In October, 1845, the Sac and Fox Indian lands were officially thrown open to white settlers.

Macaroni Cheese Deluxe
"simply delicious"

Serves 6

1¾ cups elbow macaroni, cooked
2 cups small curd cottage cheese
1 cup sour cream
1 egg, slightly beaten
3 tablespoons minced onion
2 cups shredded American cheese
¾ teaspoon salt
Dash of pepper
Paprika

Mix ingredients except paprika and put in a 2-quart greased casserole. Sprinkle with paprika. Bake at 350° for 45 minutes.

Recipes from Iowa with Love...

The wide open world of prairie and sky was overwhelming to many of the early pioneers coming into Iowa. Again and again, the prairie was described as an endless ocean or a rolling green sea where one could travel from sunup to sundown and feel one was where he had started.

Prairie Zucchini Casserole

Serves 4

3 medium zucchini, pared and sliced
1 medium onion, chopped
1 cup carrots, shredded
1 cup sour cream
1 can cream of mushroom soup
2 tablespoons butter
¾ cup herb stuffing, rolled fine

Place zucchini and onion in a greased 9×9″ baking pan. Mix carrots with sour cream and soup and spread over zucchini and onion. Mix butter and stuffing together and spread over the top. Bake at 350° for 30 minutes.

Tomato Vegetable Pie

Serves 6

Pastry for 9" pie shell
3/4 **cup chopped onion**
1 **clove garlic, crushed**
1 **tablespoon oil**
1 **17-ounce can tomatoes**
1/2 **pound zucchini, washed and thinly sliced**
2 **tablespoons finely chopped parsley**
1/4 **teaspoon basil**
3/4 **teaspoon salt**
1/8 **teaspoon pepper**
2 **eggs, beaten**
1/2 **cup shredded Cheddar cheese**

Bake pie shell 8 minutes at 425°. Saute onion and garlic in oil till tender. Add tomatoes, zucchini, herbs, salt and pepper. Simmer, uncovered, for 15 minutes. Allow to cool. Stir beaten eggs into cooled vegetables and pour into pie shell. Sprinkle with cheese, and bake at 375° for 20 minutes.

Recipes from Iowa with Love...

Special Spinach Casserole
"water chestnuts and bacon add that special crunch"

Serves 6

2 packages chopped
   frozen spinach
1 medium onion, chopped
1 8-ounce can water
   chestnuts, sliced thin
4 tablespoons butter
1 8-ounce package cream
   cheese
½ teaspoon salt
¼ teaspoon pepper
8 slices bacon, cooked
   crisp and crumbled

Cook spinach 2-3 minutes after it is thawed. Drain well. Saute onion and water chestnuts in butter. Add cream cheese, spinach, salt and pepper and mix well. Stir in half the bacon. Put the mixture into a 2-quart casserole. Sprinkle remaining bacon on top and bake at 300° for 25 minutes.

Dill Cucumbers in Sour Cream

Serves 8

2 cucumbers
1 cup red onion rings,
   thinly-sliced
¼ cup sour cream
1 tablespoon vinegar
1 teaspoon sugar
½ teaspoon salt
¼ teaspoon white pepper
2 tablespoons fresh dill,
   finely chopped
1 teaspoon chopped
   parsley

Wash and dry cucumbers and score down sides with tines of a fork. Slice thin and combine with onion rings, sour cream, vinegar, sugar, salt, white pepper and dill. Toss lightly and top with chopped parsley. Refrigerate for at least 1 hour.

Recipes from Iowa with Love...

RAGBRAI is the largest bicycling event of more than one day's duration in the world. It started 10 years ago when John Karras and Donald Kaul, two newspaper columnists for the Des Moines Register, invited anyone to join them while they spent five days bicycling across Iowa. Thousands came, ages 8 to 80, and it has become an annual production involving six to nine thousand people on bicycles and hundreds more preparing lemonade and cookies along the way.

Rosie's Barley Casserole

Serves 6

½ cup butter
2 medium onions, chopped
¾ pound mushrooms, chopped
1¼ cups pearl barley
1 small jar pimento
½ teaspoon salt
¼ teaspoon pepper
2 cups canned chicken broth
4 ounces pine nuts or slivered almonds

Melt butter in medium saucepan and saute onions and mushrooms. Add barley and cook until barley is a delicate brown. Add pimento, salt and pepper; mix. Put into a 2-quart casserole, add chicken broth and spread nuts on top. Cover and bake at 350° for 1½ hours.

Cabbage with Sour Cream
"quick and tasty"

Serves 8-10

1 **medium head green
   cabbage**
3 **tablespoons bacon
   drippings**
1 **8-ounce carton sour
   cream**
   Salt and pepper to taste

Slice cabbage very thin. Saute in bacon drippings 8 minutes. Stir in sour cream and warm thoroughly. Season with salt and pepper to taste. Serve immediately.

Recipes from Iowa with Love...

On warm summer nights when all is quiet except for the song of the crickets, Iowa farmers claim they can hear the corn grow. The plants grow three to five inches a day at the peak of the growing season.

Garden Roundup Vegetables

"colorful, quick and low in calories"

Serves 4

1½ tablespoons oil
1 large carrot, sliced
1 large rib celery, sliced
1 cup fresh broccoli,
   in bite-size pieces
½ cup sliced onion
½ cup sliced mushrooms
¼ cup chicken broth
   Salt and pepper to taste

Heat the oil in a large skillet until hot but not smoking. Add vegetables and stir until coated with oil. Add chicken broth and cover skillet for 5-8 minutes. Season and serve.

Vegetables used may vary according to what is available. Cauliflower, green pepper and zucchini are all successful additions.

Vegetable Buffet Dish

Serves 6-8

1 **10-ounce package frozen
   lima beans**
1 **10-ounce package frozen
   green beans**
1 **10-ounce package frozen
   green peas**
1½ **cups mayonnaise-style
   salad dressing**
1 **teaspoon prepared
   mustard**
1 **small onion, diced**
3 **hard-cooked eggs,
   chopped**
1 **teaspoon Worcestershire
   sauce**
   Dash red pepper sauce

Cook frozen vegetables according to package directions and drain. Combine remaining ingredients for the sauce and stir into the vegetables. Place in oiled 1½-quart baking dish. Bake at 325° for 30 minutes.

The number of Iowa counties with Indian names indicates the extent of Indian influence in early Iowa history. We have Black Hawk, Winnebago, Pottawattamie, Mahaska, Poweshiek, Cherokee, Keokuk, Allamakee, Appanoose, Chickasaw, Monona, Pocahontas, Wapello, Winneshiek, Sac, Sioux, Osceola, and Tama.

Celery-Almond Casserole

Serves 6-8

4 cups celery, cut in
    1-inch pieces
½ teaspoon salt
1 cup slivered almonds
1 10¾-ounce can cream of
    chicken soup
½ cup sour cream
1 8-ounce can water
    chestnuts, drained
    and sliced
   Buttered soft bread
    crumbs

Cook celery in small amount of boiling water, with salt, until tender but still crisp. Drain. Toast almonds in 325° oven 5-10 minutes or until lightly browned. Add with remaining ingredients, except crumbs. Bake uncovered at 350° for 30 minutes.

Iowa ranks second in the production of soybeans, producing about 16 percent of the nation's supply. The soybean is recognized as a "food of the future" because it is high in protein and low in carbohydrates. Its sprouts are very tender and crisp and are a good addition to omelets, salads, stews and vegetable casseroles.

Soybean Sprouts

1 pound soybeans
(mung variety)
3 pints water

Soak beans in water overnight. Put them in a container large enough to allow them to expand 6 times. If using a large glass jar, cover opening with a piece of cloth and tie it on. Keep in a warm, dark place; flood with lukewarm water 4 or 5 times each day and drain each time. Sprouts will be 2 to 3 inches long in 4 to 6 days. Store in the refrigerator.

Carrot Ring

"attractive and serves as both a bread and a vegetable"

Serves 8

¼ **cup fine bread crumbs**
1 **scant cup shortening**
¼ **cup brown sugar**
1 **egg, beaten**
1 **cup grated carrots**
1¼ **cups flour**
1 **teaspoon salt**
1 **teaspoon baking powder**
1 **teaspoon soda**
2 **teaspoons lemon juice**
1 **tablespoon cold water**

Oil a 5½ cup ring mold. Sprinkle half the bread crumbs in ring mold. Mix ingredients in order given. Pour mixture into ring mold, and sprinkle remaining bread crumbs on top. Bake at 350° for 35-40 minutes, or until carrot ring pulls away from sides of pan. Unmold and serve with mushroom sauce.

Mushroom Sauce
1 **can golden mushroom soup**
1 **small can mushrooms**
1 **teaspoon kitchen bouquet flavoring**
Salt and pepper to taste

Mix all ingredients and bring to a boil.

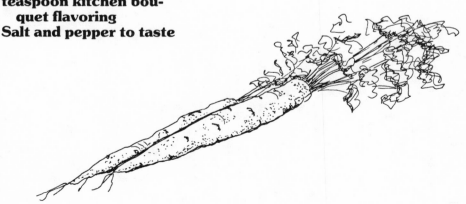

Des Moines' Drake University is the home of the famed Drake Relays. This major intercollegiate and invitational track event draws outstanding teams and individuals from thoughout the United States.

Mustard Ring
"unusual... and delicious with ham"

Serves 6

4 eggs
1 cup water
½ cup vinegar
¾ cup sugar
1½ tablespoons dry mustard
¼ teaspoon salt
1 envelope unflavored gelatin
½ teaspoon tumeric
½ pint whipping cream
¾ cup finely chopped celery
2 tablespoons capers
Parsley

Beat eggs in top of double boiler. Add water and vinegar. Mix sugar, mustard, salt, gelatin and tumeric together; add to egg mixture. Cook until slightly thickened. Cool. Whip cream until stiff. Fold celery, capers and whipped cream into egg mixture. Spoon into a lightly oiled 1½-quart ring mold. Chill for 3-4 hours. To serve, unmold and garnish with parsley.

Recipes from Iowa with Love...

Amelia Bloomer, whose name was given to the controversial baggy pantaloons worn by "liberated" women of the middle of the last century, was a pioneer in the struggle for women's rights. She moved to Council Bluffs when she was 37, and continued to work for women's right to vote.

Marinated Mushrooms

Serves 8

⅔ cup tarragon vinegar
½ cup oil
1 garlic clove, crushed
1 tablespoon sugar
1 teaspoon salt
⅛ teaspoon pepper
2 tablespoons water
1 medium onion, sliced
2 pints fresh mushrooms

Combine all ingredients but onion and mushrooms. Pour over onion and mushrooms in glass bowl. Allow to marinate overnight.

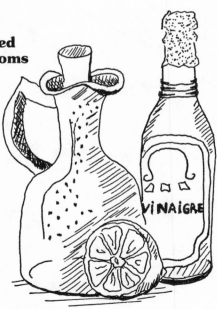

Turkey Dressing Supreme

Serves 12

2 8-ounce packages
   stuffing mix
1 package onion soup mix
2 cans chicken rice soup
1 can water
2 3-ounce cans mushrooms,
   drained
1 can mushroom steak
   sauce
1 can water chestnuts,
   drained, diced
1 cup melted butter
1 teaspoon salt
2 teaspoons herb-flavored
   seasoning salt
6 eggs, slightly beaten
2 cups chopped celery,
   cooked
1 tablespoon thyme

Mix all ingredients together cold. Yield is enough for a 25-pound turkey. Extra stuffing may be frozen either before or after baking for future use.

Recipes from Iowa with Love...

Every September, Mount Pleasant hosts the Midwest Old Threshers Annual Reunion...a festival of the steam era. The reunion features steam trains, steam engines, vintage tractors, antique cars and other exhibits of a bygone era. Visitors come to reminisce, to learn of their heritage and to enjoy the craft shows and the top country entertainment which is part of the get-together.

Sweet Potatoes Supreme

"from the Old Threshers' Cookbook"

Serves 6

3 cups canned sweet
    potatoes
¼ cup milk
⅓ cup margarine, melted
1 teaspoon vanilla
2 eggs, beaten

Topping
1 cup coconut
1 cup firmly packed
    brown sugar
⅓ cup all-purpose flour
⅓ cup margarine, melted
1 cup pecans, chopped

Drain liquid from sweet potatoes. Mash. Mix with milk, margarine, vanilla, and eggs. Spoon into a lightly greased 8″ square baking dish.

Combine topping ingredients. Sprinkle over the top of the sweet potatoes. Bake at 375° oven for 25 minutes.

MIDWEST OLD THRESHERS
ANNUAL REUNION*
* FIVE DAYS ENDING LABOR DAY
MOUNT PLEASANT, IOWA

Many have contributed to the evolution of hybrid corn, but Henry Wallace was the first to commercialize the results of his findings. He became a founder of the company that is now Pioneer Hi-Bred International, Inc., one of Iowa's largest corporations. Mr. Wallace was vice-president of the United States from 1941-45.

Iowa Corn Pudding

Serves 6

2 **tablespoons sugar**
1 **teaspoon salt**
3 **eggs, slightly beaten**
2 **tablespoons finely
     chopped onion**
2 **tablespoons flour**
2 **cups milk**
1 **13-ounce can evaporated
     milk**
3 **cups fresh or frozen corn**
2 **tablespoons butter**

Beat sugar and salt into eggs. Add remaining ingredients and pour into a 2-quart casserole. Bake at 350° for 1 hour or until set.

Recipes from Iowa with Love...

The Amish community near Kalona is one of the strictest of the groups of Old Order Amish. The settlers are called "plain people" and live simply, with little change from generation to generation. Modern conveniences are rejected and horse-drawn buggies are used for transportation.

Amish Baby Pearl Tapioca

"served as a side dish with the main course at Amish dinners"

Serves 8

5 cups water
¼ teaspoon salt
½ cup sugar
1 cup baby pearl tapioca
1 tablespoon strawberry
    gelatin
1 cup whipped cream,
    whipped
  Bananas, pineapple or
    other fruit, sliced

Bring water to a boil and add salt, sugar, and tapioca. Cook 10-12 minutes, or until clear. Add gelatin; stir, and cool. When cool, fold in whipped cream and fruit of your preference.

Sweets
and
Treats

Harvest Apple Cake

"a family recipe from one of Iowa's finest cooks"

Serves 18

2 cups sugar
½ cup butter or margarine
2 eggs, beaten
2 cups flour
1 teaspoon soda
3 teaspoons cinnamon
½ teaspoon nutmeg
1 teaspoon salt
1 cup chopped walnuts
4 cups finely chopped
    apples

Cream sugar and butter together, add eggs and mix. Sift dry ingredients together, add to batter and blend. Stir in nuts and apples. Pour into a greased 9×13″ pan and bake at 350° for 15 minutes. Reduce heat to 300° and bake for 45 minutes. Serve warm with Harvest Cake Sauce.

Harvest Cake Sauce
1 cup sugar
½ cup butter (do not
    substitute margarine)
½ cup half and half
    (light cream)
1 teaspoon vanilla

Cook together over low heat, stirring constantly, until mixture coats the spoon. Serve warm.

Seven "old world" villages make up the Amana Colonies. When they were established in 1855, they were spaced "one hour by oxen" apart. The German families who formed the colonies lived a communal life sharing their wealth, their cooking, and their religion. The old ways have mostly been abandoned, but visitors are charmed by the old world atmosphere.

Chocolate Bit Almond Cake
"looks its most elegant in a footed glass cake server"

6 egg whites
1 cup sugar
6 egg yolks
1 teaspoon vanilla
¾ cup sifted flour
1 teaspoon baking powder
20 almonds, finely chopped
2 squares unsweetened baking chocolate, grated (reserve 1 tablespoon for decoration)
2 cups whipping cream
6 tablespoons sugar
1 teaspoon vanilla

Beat egg whites until stiff; add half the sugar and mix. Set aside. Beat egg yolks until lemon-colored and frothy; add rest of sugar and vanilla. Mix. Sift flour and baking powder into the egg yolk mixture and fold in. Add almonds and chocolate; mix. Fold into egg white mixture. Transfer to ungreased angel food cake pan and bake at 350° for 40 minutes. Invert in pan to cool. Remove from pan and slice in 3 layers. Whip cream until it forms mounds. Add sugar and vanilla and beat until stiff. Fill between layers and frost with whipped cream. Decorate top with reserved grated chocolate.

Harvest time meant extra people for Iowa farm women to feed. This recipe came from a farm-wife who enjoyed serving it to the appreciative crew who came to help harvest the crops.

Banana Marshmallow Cake
"during baking, marshmallows melt like flowers over top of cake"

Makes 18 pieces

2½ cups sugar
1 cup shortening
4 egg whites
3 cups flour
1½ teaspoons baking powder
2 cups mashed bananas
6 tablespoons buttermilk
    or sour milk
1 teaspoon vanilla
¾ cup nuts (optional)
¾ cup raisins (optional)
16 marshmallows

Cream sugar and shortening together in a large bowl. Add rest of ingredients, except marshmallows and mix thoroughly. Place marshmallows in a greased and floured 9×13" pan in rows 2" apart. Pour batter over the marshmallows. Smack pan smartly on counter until tops of marshmallows show through batter. Bake at 350° for 1 hour.

Recipes from Iowa with Love...

"Iowa's black soil probably has a greater value than all the silver and gold mines in the entire world," according to the World Book Encyclopedia. Glaciers moving across the northern and central portions of Iowa planed the land and left deposits that became some of the richest topsoil in the world.

Chocolate Chip Date Cake

"a valuable recipe according to friends of this Iowa cook"

Serves 15

1 cup boiling water
1 cup chopped dates
1 teaspoon soda
1 cup sugar
½ cup butter
½ cup shortening
2 eggs, beaten
1¾ cups sifted flour
1½ tablespoons cocoa
½ teaspoon salt
½ teaspoon soda
1 teaspoon vanilla
1 cup chocolate chips
½ cup chopped nuts
¼ cup sugar

Pour water over dates and 1 teaspoon soda. Let cool. Cream 1 cup sugar, butter and shortening. Add eggs and date mixture. Sift flour, cocoa, salt and ½ teaspoon soda and add to batter. Add vanilla and ½ cup chocolate chips. Pour into a greased 9×13" pan. Mix remaining chips, nuts and ¼ cup sugar together and sprinkle over top of the batter. This will make a frosting as it bakes. Place in a 350° oven for 35 minutes.

Chautauqua parks are found in a number of Iowa towns. Chautauquas were a prime source of family entertainment before the era of radio and television. The traveling troupes would set up a large tent in the local park and offer programs that included music, drama and lectures on a variety of subjects.

Chocolate Cake Chautauqua

"simple to make sheetcake"

Serves 12

½ cup margarine
1 cup water
½ cup shortening
4 tablespoons cocoa
2 cups flour
2 cups sugar
½ cup buttermilk
2 eggs
¼ teaspoon salt
1 teaspoon vanilla
1 teaspoon soda

Place margarine, water and shortening in a small saucepan and bring to a boil. In a large bowl, mix the cocoa, flour and sugar. Pour the hot mixture over the dry ingredients and stir. Add remaining ingredients, mix well; pour into a greased 10×15″ cake pan. Bake at 400° for 20 minutes. Ten minutes before cake is done, make frosting.

Frosting
½ cup margarine
4 tablespoons cocoa
5 tablespoons milk
1 teaspoon vanilla
3- 3½ cups powdered sugar
1 cup chopped pecans
   (optional)

Bring margarine, cocoa and milk to a boil in a small saucepan. Remove from heat and add vanilla, powdered sugar and pecans, if desired. Beat together and spread over hot cake.

Pumpkin Cake

"especially good served with whipped cream while warm"

Serves 12

1 cup margarine
3 cups sugar
3 eggs
2½ cups flour
1 teaspoon salt
1 teaspoon cinnamon
1 teaspoon nutmeg
1 teaspoon soda
½ teaspoon baking powder
2 cups canned pumpkin
1 teaspoon vanilla

Cream margarine and sugar. Add eggs one at a time, beating after each addition. Sift dry ingredients together. Add to egg mixture, alternating with pumpkin. Add vanilla and mix well. Bake in a greased and floured tube or bundt pan at 325° for 1½ hours.

Recipes from Iowa with Love…

The Meredith Corporation of Des Moines has sold over 22,000,000 copies of *"Better Homes and Gardens New Cook Book"* since it was first introduced in 1930. This Cheesecake Supreme recipe is from their Ninth Edition, 1982.

Cheesecake Supreme

Serves 12

¾ cup all-purpose flour
3 tablespoons sugar
1 teaspoon finely shred-
    ded lemon peel
6 tablespoons butter or
    margarine
1 slightly beaten egg yolk
½ teaspoon vanilla
3 8-ounce packages cream
    cheese, softened
1 cup sugar
2 tablespoons all-purpose
    flour
¼ teaspoon salt
2 eggs
1 egg yolk
¼ cup milk
    Cherry Sauce

To prepare crust, combine the ¾ cup flour, the 3 tablespoons sugar, and ½ teaspoon of the lemon peel. Cut in butter or margarine till crumbly. Stir in 1 slightly beaten egg yolk and ¼ teaspoon of the vanilla. Pat ⅓ of the dough onto the bottom of an 8- or 9-inch springform pan (with sides removed). Bake in a 400° oven for 7 minutes or till golden; cool.

Butter the sides of pan, attach to bottom. Pat remaining dough onto sides of pan to a height of 1¾-inches; set aside.

For the filling, in a large mixer bowl beat together the softened cream cheese, remaining lemon peel, and remaining vanilla till fluffy. Stir together the 1 cup sugar, the 2 tablespoons flour, and the salt; gradually stir into cream cheese mixture. Add the 2 eggs and 1 egg yolk all at once, beating at low speed just till combined. Stir in milk. Turn into crust-lined pan. Bake in a 450° oven for 10 minutes. Reduce heat to 300°; bake 50 to 55 minutes more or till center appears set and a knife comes out clean. Cool 15 minutes. Loosen sides of cheesecake from pan with a spatula. Cool 30 minutes; remove sides of pan. Cool about 2 hours longer. Chill thoroughly. Top with Cherry Sauce. Serves 12.

CHERRY SAUCE: in a sauce pan combine ¾ cup sugar, 2 tablespoons cornstarch and a dash of salt. Stir in ⅓ cup water. Stir in 4 cups fresh or frozen unsweetened pitted tart red cherries, thawed. Cook and stir 1 to 2 minutes more. Cover; chill without stirring. (Or, use one 21-ounce can cherry pie filling instead of sauce.)

Holiday Cake

"a tradition at Easter and other holidays for one Iowa family"

Serves 12

1 (2-layer) package of yellow cake mix
¾ cup apricot nectar
¾ cup oil
4 eggs
1 3-ounce package lemon gelatin
Juice of 2 fresh lemons
1½ cups powdered sugar

Combine cake mix, apricot nectar, oil, eggs and gelatin plus 1 tablespoon of the lemon juice. Mix well. Pour into oiled and floured bundt pan. Bake at 350° for 10 minutes; lower heat to 325° and bake for 55 minutes or until done. Remove cake from pan, and while it is still warm, pour a glaze of powdered sugar mixed with lemon juice over the top of cake. Glaze will soak into the cake.

Recipes from Iowa with Love...

The "Waterloo Boy" was the name given to a gasoline traction engine that was developed in 1892 by a Waterloo company. It was so well received by farmers in the area that the John Deere Company of Moline, Ill., purchased the company and made Waterloo the center for its tractor production.

Christmas Fruit Cake

2 cups sugar
1 cup margarine
4 eggs
½ cup buttermilk
1 teaspoon soda
2 cups chopped dates
1 14-ounce package flaked
   coconut
1 pound candy orange
   slices, chopped
3½ cups flour
1 teaspoon baking powder
1 teaspoon vanilla
2 cups chopped nuts
1 cup green and red
   candied cherries,
   chopped

Cream sugar and margarine. Add eggs and mix well. Add remaining ingredients and blend. Pour into a greased and floured bundt pan and bake at 250° for 2½-3 hours.

The University of Okoboji wasn't founded, it just happened. It is a very liberal arts college of the imagination whose campus extends from the northern tip of Big Spirit Lake to Milford and includes all of lakes West Okoboji and East Okoboji. Its main goal is to provide year-round fun for students and alumni, which includes everyone who lives in the area or enjoys the recreational activities provided by the area.

Fudge-Mint Pie

"scrumptious combination – and easy to make"

Serves 7

1 9" baked pie shell
1 small package instant chocolate fudge pudding mix
1½ cups milk
1 small package French vanilla pudding mix
1¼ cups milk
¼ cup creme de menthe
½ cup whipping cream
2 tablespoons sugar
½ teaspoon vanilla
1 tablespoon shaved semi-sweet chocolate

Allow pie shell to cool. Beat fudge pudding mix with 1½ cups milk for 1 minute. Pour into pie shell and chill. Beat French vanilla pudding mix with 1¼ cups milk and creme de menthe for 1 minute. Pour over chocolate pudding and chill till set. Whip the cream with sugar and vanilla until stiff. Frost the pie with whipped cream and sprinkle with chocolate.

Sour Cream Raisin Pie

"Elmer's favorite"

1 cup sugar
1 large tablespoon flour
1 teaspoon cinnamon
1 teaspoon nutmeg
1 cup sour cream
2 egg yolks
½ cup raisins
½ cup chopped nuts
1 baked single pie crust
2 egg whites
¼ teaspoon vanilla
2 tablespoons sugar

Mix 1 cup sugar, flour and spices in a saucepan. Add sour cream, egg yolks and raisins. Cook over medium heat until thick and shiny. Add nuts and pour into pie shell. Beat egg whites with vanilla until soft peaks form. Gradually add sugar until it all is dissolved. Bake at 350° for 12-15 minutes.

Recipes from Iowa with Love...

The Iowa State Fair is the nation's premier agriculture and livestock fair. Native Iowan Phil Stong used it as the background for his novel, *State Fair*, which was later made into a movie of the same name. Good cooks from all over Iowa bring mouth-watering examples of their specialties to be judged in the foods competition. It truly becomes a showcase for the bounty of Iowa.

Lemon Meringue Pie (Italian Meringue)

"this is a winner"

Serves 6-7

1¼ **cups sugar**
6 **tablespoons cornstarch**
   Pinch of salt
2 **cups boiling water**
1 **teaspoon grated lemon rind**
¼ **cup butter**
3 **egg yolks, slightly beaten**
½ **cup lemon juice**
1 **9" baked pie shell**

Mix sugar, cornstarch and salt in a saucepan. Add boiling water and lemon rind. Cook over medium heat, stirring constantly, until thickened. Continue cooking, stirring frequently, about 20 minutes, or until no taste of cornstarch remains. Remove from heat, add butter, and pour hot mixture slowly over egg yolks and lemon juice. Beat until smooth. Return to heat until mixture becomes steaming hot. Pour into pie shell and bake at 400° for 5 minutes. Top with Italian Meringue.

   Italian Meringue
3 **egg whites**
   Pinch of salt
¼ **teaspoon cream of tartar**
1⅓ **cups sugar**
½ **cup water**

Beat egg whites until foamy; add salt and cream of tartar. Beat until mixture forms stiff, shining peaks. Set aside. Combine sugar and water in saucepan and set over high heat. Swirl pan gently by handle until sugar has dissolved and liquid is clear. Cover pan and boil rapidly for a few seconds; uncover and boil rapidly to soft-ball stage. While beating egg whites, pour sugar syrup over them in a thin stream. Continue beating for at least 5 minutes, or until mixture cools. Spread over lemon mixture and bake at 350° for 15 minutes.

Frosty Lemonade Pie

"the peanut butter flavor in the crust is just right with the tangy filling"

Serves 6-7

Crust
1²/₃ **cups crushed peanut butter flavored cereal**
¹/₃ **cup firmly packed brown sugar**
¹/₃ **cup soft butter or margarine**

Combine ingredients and mix thoroughly. Reserve ¼ cup to garnish top of pie. Press remaining mixture firmly into 9" pie pan. Bake at 350° for 5-8 minutes. Cool and freeze.

Filling
1 **6-ounce can frozen lemonade concentrate**
1 **quart vanilla ice cream Thin lemon slices**

Allow lemonade concentrate and ice cream to thaw just enough to mix easily. Spread in pie shell and garnish with reserved crumbs and lemon slices.

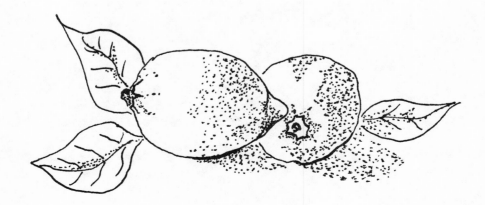

Fresh Peach Cream Pie
"makes a cream filling with a golden brown top"

1 unbaked 9" pie shell
4 or 5 fresh peaches, sliced
1 scant cup sugar
¼ cup flour
¼ teaspoon nutmeg
1 cup whipping cream

Line unbaked pie shell with 1 layer only of fresh peaches. Mix sugar, flour and nutmeg; sprinkle over peaches. Pour whipping cream over peaches. Bake at 400° for 10 minutes; lower heat to 350° and bake 50-60 minutes or until brown and bubbly.

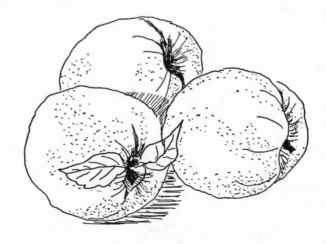

Fresh Strawberry Pie

"a 'must' during strawberry season"

Serves 6

1 quart fresh strawberries
1 baked 9" pie shell
1 cup sugar
3 tablespoons cornstarch
½ cup water
  A few drops red food
    coloring (optional)
2 tablespoons lemon juice

Wash strawberries and remove stems; reserve 6 of the nicest berries to garnish pie. Use 1½ cups to line pie shell. Mash remaining strawberries and combine with sugar, cornstarch and water in medium saucepan. Stir and cook about 4 minutes or until clear. Add a few drops of red food coloring if desired. Remove from heat; add lemon juice. Cool and pour over strawberries in pie shell. Refrigerate 3 hours. Serve with whipped cream and garnish with reserved strawberries.

"Iowa Pride" Chess Pie
"delicious warm or chilled"

Serves 6

1 cup granulated sugar
½ cup light brown sugar, firmly packed
1 tablespoon flour
1 tablespoon yellow cornmeal
⅛ teaspoon salt
3 large eggs
½ cup melted butter
3 tablespoons milk or light cream
1½ teaspoons white vinegar
1 teaspoon vanilla
1 unbaked 9" pie shell, (or plain or butter-flavored ready crust)

Toss sugars, flour, cornmeal and salt together with a fork. Add eggs, melted butter, milk or cream, vinegar and vanilla. Beat mixture with electric beater until smooth. Pour into unbaked pie shell. Cover edges of crust with narrow strips of foil for first 25 minutes of baking to prevent overbrowning. Bake at 350° for 35-40 minutes or until a clean knife inserted in the center comes out clean. Can be frozen.

Chocolate Roll
"a special dessert... worth the time involved"

Serves 8

6 **egg whites**
½ **teaspoon cream of tartar**
½ **cup sugar**
6 **egg yolks**
½ **cup sugar**
4 **tablespoons cocoa**
4 **tablespoons sifted flour**
½ **teaspoon salt**
1 **teaspoon vanilla**

Whipped Cream Filling
½ **teaspoon gelatin**
½ **tablespoon warm milk**
½ **pint whipping cream**
¼ **cup sifted powdered
   sugar**
1 **teaspoon vanilla**

Chocolate Gloss
½ **cup sugar**
1½ **tablespoons cornstarch**
1 **1-ounce square un-
   sweetened chocolate,
   grated**
¼ **teaspoon salt**
½ **cup boiling water**
1½ **tablespoons butter**
½ **teaspoon vanilla**

Beat egg whites and cream of tartar until stiff. Gradually add ½ cup sugar and beat till glossy. Set aside. Beat egg yolks until thick; beat in ½ cup sugar. Sift the dry ingredients together and beat into yolk mixture. Stir in the vanilla. Gently fold into the egg white mixture and spread into a 10×15" pan that is lined with greased waxed paper. Bake at 325° for 20-25 minutes or until cake springs back when lightly touched. Quickly turn upside down onto a clean towel sprinkled with powdered sugar. Immediately remove waxed paper and roll up lengthwise with towel. About 1 hour before serving unroll and fill with Whipped Cream Filling.

To make filling, soften gelatin in warm milk. Beat whipping cream till stiff, beat in sugar, vanilla and gelatin. Spread on chocolate sponge layer and roll up carefully.

Top with Chocolate Gloss. To make gloss, mix sugar, cornstarch, chocolate and salt. Add water and cook until mixture thickens. Remove from heat and add butter and vanilla. Spread on top of chocolate roll while gloss is still warm.

Caramel Layer Chocolate Squares
"simple to make — delicious to eat"

Makes 20 squares

1 14-ounce package
   caramels
1/3 cup evaporated milk
3/4 cup butter, melted
1 package German
   chocolate cake mix
1 cup chopped nuts
1/3 cup evaporated milk
1 cup chocolate chips

Combine caramels and 1/3 cup evaporated milk in heavy saucepan. Cook over low heat, stirring constantly until caramels are melted. Set aside. Grease and flour 9×13" pan. Combine melted butter, dry cake mix, nuts and evaporated milk in large bowl and mix. Press half the dough in pan, reserving other half for topping. Bake at 350° for 6 minutes. Sprinkle chocolate chips on baked portion and spread caramel mixture evenly over chips. Crumble reserved dough mixture over caramel. Return to oven and bake 15 to 18 minutes. Cool. Refrigerate 30 minutes to set caramel. Cut into squares.

Recipes from Iowa with Love...

General Grenville Dodge was called "the greatest railroad builder of all time" because of his role as chief construction engineer for the Union Pacific Railroad. He went on to outstanding success as a major general during the Civil War. He was captivated with the West and built a 14-room mansion in Council Bluffs overlooking the Missouri Valley. The General Dodge House is now maintained as a public museum.

Chocolate Nut Kisses

"an outstanding success"

Makes 40 cookies

1 cup butter or margarine
½ cup powdered sugar
1 teaspoon vanilla
2 cups flour
¼ teaspoon salt
1 cup finely chopped
    pecans
40 chocolate candy kisses
    Additional powdered
    sugar

Using an electric mixer, cream butter and powdered sugar together until light and fluffy. Add vanilla. Gradually sift flour and salt into butter mixture and blend with mixer at low speed. When thoroughly blended, add pecans. Grease hands and form balls of dough around chocolate kisses. Place on ungreased cookie sheets and bake at 375° for 11-12 minutes. Roll in powdered sugar while warm.

Thousands of tourists flock to Pella each May for the town's annual Tulip Time. The streets and sidewalks are lined with a dazzling display of spring flowers, and visitors are treated to folk dances, delicious authentic pastries, and shops filled with antiques and crafts of Dutch heritage.

Dutch Letters
"from the Pella Collector's Cookbook"

Makes 14 pieces

2 cups butter
4 cups flour
1 cup water

Combine butter and flour. Stir in water and mix well. Chill overnight or longer.

Almond Filling
1 pound almond paste
2 cups sugar
3 eggs
1 teaspoon vanilla
1 egg white, beaten
   Sugar

Using an electric mixer, beat almond paste until smooth. Add sugar, eggs and vanilla to the paste; mix thoroughly and chill.

When ready to bake, divide dough and filling each into 14 parts. Roll each section of dough into a 4×14" strip. Take a portion of filling and spread down center of dough strip. Lap one side of dough over filling, then other side, and pinch ends shut. Repeat. Place on a greased cookie sheet with seams on bottom. Brush tops with egg white and sprinkle with sugar. Prick with fork every 2" to let steam escape. Bake at 400° for 30 minutes.

Recipes from Iowa with Love...

Mark Twain lived and worked in Keokuk in the 1850's. One of his most famous books, *Life on the Mississippi*, testifies to his lifelong fascination with the river and the towns that grew up along its banks.

Mississippi Mud Bars
"very rich"

Makes 48 pieces

1 cup butter
2 cups sugar
4 eggs
2 tablespoons cocoa
2 teaspoons vanilla
1½ cups flour
1⅓ cups coconut
1½ cups chopped nuts
1 8-ounce jar marshmallow
    cream

Cream butter and sugar. Add eggs, cocoa and vanilla. Add flour and mix well. Fold in the coconut and nuts. Bake in a greased and floured 9×13" pan at 350° for 35 minutes. Spread with marshmallow cream while still hot. Cool completely before frosting.

Frosting
1 1-pound box powdered
    sugar
½ cup butter
½ cup evaporated milk
⅓ cup cocoa
1 teaspoon vanilla

Mix frosting ingredients together and beat until smooth. Spread over the marshmallow cream. Cut into 1½×1½" pieces.

A chance seedling apple tree grew in an orchard belonging to Amos Hiatt in Madison County. The fruit from this tree was so sweet that it was called "delicious". From this tree the Delicious apple was developed, and more than ten million trees throughout the world have come from its stock.

Delicious Applesauce Spice Bars

Makes 24 bars

2   cups flour, sifted
2   teaspoons soda
¾   teaspoon cinnamon
¼   teaspoon cloves
¼   teaspoon nutmeg
½   teaspoon salt
½   cup soft butter
1   cup sugar
1   egg
1   teaspoon vanilla
1½ cups applesauce
1   cup pecans
1   cup raisins

Caramel Frosting
½   cup butter
1   cup brown sugar
¼   cup milk
2   cups powdered sugar
1   teaspoon vanilla
    Dash of salt

Sift first six ingredients together. Mix butter and sugar together and add flour mixture and rest of the ingredients. Pour into 9×13" pan and bake at 350° for 25 minutes. Cool and frost with Caramel Frosting.

Cook butter and sugar for 2 minutes. Add milk and just bring to a boil. Add powdered sugar, vanilla and salt and beat until spreading consistency. Spread over top of Applesauce Bars.

Recipes from Iowa with Love...

The golden dome of the Iowa State Capitol dominates the skyline of Des Moines. The dome is covered with 23-carat gold leaf and is said to be the largest gold dome in the country. For years, climbing the spiral staircase to the very top was considered the only way to become an Iowan if you were not born here. The topmost part is no longer open to the public because of safety precautions.

Golden Apricot Bars

"tangy apricot flavor for a dessert that's not too sweet"

Makes 48 bars

12 ounces dried apricots
1 cup soft butter
½ cup sugar
2⅔ cups flour
1 teaspoon baking powder
½ teaspoon salt
2 cups firmly packed
    brown sugar
4 eggs, beaten
1 teaspoon vanilla
1 cup chopped walnuts

Rinse apricots. Cover with water and boil 10 minutes. Drain, cool and chop. Mix butter, sugar and 2 cups flour until crumbly. Press into a greased 9×13" pan and bake at 350° for 25 minutes. Sift remaining ⅔ cup flour, baking powder and salt. Beat brown sugar into eggs, and mix in apricots, vanilla, nuts and flour mixture. Spread over baked layer and bake at 350° for 35 minutes. May be sprinkled with powdered sugar, if desired.

Recipes from Iowa with Love...

Several covered bridges can be seen in Madison County near Winterset. A source of delight to painters and photographers, these wooden structures served a multitude of purposes. They protected travelers during rainstorms, offered a secluded spot for romantic couples, served as billboards for local merchants, and were used as churches by early circuit riding ministers.

Winterset Raisin Bars

Makes 24 bars

1½ cups flour
1 teaspoon baking powder
1 cup brown sugar
1½ cups quick oatmeal
¾ cup butter

Filling
2 cups raisins
1½ cups hot water
1 cup sugar
2 tablespoons flour
1 teaspoon cinnamon
½ teaspoon ground cloves
1 teaspoon vinegar
1 tablespoon butter

Sift flour and baking powder together. Add brown sugar, oatmeal and butter and work together until thoroughly mixed. Press ⅔ of this mixture into a greased and floured 9×13" pan.

Boil ingredients for raisin filling in a sauce pan, stirring constantly, until thickened (about 5 minutes). Spread over crumb mixture in the pan. Cover with the remaining crumb mixture and bake at 350° for 35-40 minutes.

Lemon Bars

Makes 24 pieces

Crust
2 cups flour
½ cup powdered sugar
1 cup soft butter

Filling
4 eggs
2 cups sugar
6 tablespoons lemon juice
Grated rind of 1 lemon
1 teaspoon baking powder
2 tablespoons flour

Mix flour, powdered sugar and butter together and pat into a 9×13″ cake pan. Bake crust at 350° degrees for 20 minutes.

Beat together eggs, sugar, lemon juice, rind, baking powder and flour until thoroughly mixed. Pour over baked crust and bake 20-25 minutes. Sprinkle with powdered sugar when cool and cut into 24 bars.

Living History Farms is a 600-acre outdoor agricultural museum featuring five different time periods and tracing the development of farming, homesteads, trades and towns. The different sites show an Ioway Indian Village of about the year 1700, and 1849 Pioneer Farm, a Victorian town called Walnut Hill, a 1900 Farm and the Farm of Today and Tomorrow. The museum is located just off the interstate in northwest Des Moines.

Cry Babies

**"a soft ginger cookie recipe from Living History Farms
A Pictorial History of Food in Iowa"**

1 **cup butter**	Cream butter and sugar together. Add egg, molasses, milk and dry ingredients which have been sifted together. Drop by teaspoon onto greased cookie sheet. Bake at 350° for 15-20 minutes.
1 **cup sugar**	
1 **egg**	
1 **cup molasses**	
1 **cup milk**	
4 **cups flour**	
1 **teaspoon soda**	
1 **teaspoon ginger**	

Recipes from Iowa with Love...

The first washing machine built by the Maytag Company in Newton was called the "Pastime" model. The year was 1907, and it was the first step in freeing women from the drudgery of washing clothes by hand. Today, Newton is called "the washing machine center of the world."

Potato Chip Cookies
"light and crisp"

Makes 36 cookies

1 cup margarine
½ cup sugar
1 teaspoon vanilla
1½ cups flour
1 cup coarsely crushed
    potato chips
¾ cup chopped nuts
    Powdered sugar

Cream butter and sugar together and add vanilla. Add flour and work into mixture until blended. Add potato chips and nuts and mix thoroughly. Form into balls the size of walnuts, place on ungreased cookie sheet and flatten with hand. Bake at 350° for 10 minutes. Sprinkle with sieved powdered sugar while slightly warm.

Recipes from Iowa with Love...

In 1872, a young man named Robert Stuart visited eastern Iowa and realized that the eight-foot deep topsoil, the cool springs and the hot summers were what he needed to grow oats of the highest quality. He moved the family business to Cedar Rapids, starting the company that later became Quaker Oats, one of the largest cereal companies in the world.

Oatmeal Lace Cookies
"thin and crisp"

Makes 96 cookies

½ cup butter
1 cup plus 2 tablespoons firmly packed brown sugar
1 medium egg, slightly beaten
1 teaspoon vanilla
½ teaspoon salt
3½ cups quick-cooking oats

Cream butter and sugar. Beat in egg, vanilla and salt. Add oats and blend thoroughly. Drop by ½-teaspoons 3" apart on greased cookie sheets. Flatten slightly with back of spoon. Bake at 325° for 8-10 minutes.

Old Fashioned QUAKER OATS

Recipes from Iowa with Love...

Grant Wood is the artist most closely associated with Iowa. His widely known *American Gothic* shows a solemn farm couple standing in front of their farm home. When a critic suggested that such people did not exist, Mr. Wood replied that the models were his relatives.

Mary's Oatmeal Chocolate Chip Cookies
"an all-time favorite recipe"

Makes about 4 dozen

1 cup butter
1 cup brown sugar, firmly packed
1 cup granulated sugar
2 eggs, beaten
2 cups quick oatmeal
1 teaspoon vanilla
2 cups sifted flour
1 teaspoon soda
½ teaspoon salt
¼ cup wheat germ
¼ cup chopped pecans
1 cup chocolate chips

Cream butter and sugars thoroughly; add eggs, oatmeal and vanilla. Mix. Add sifted flour, soda and salt; add wheat germ, pecans and chocolate chips. Mix. Drop by spoonfuls on greased cookie sheets. Bake in 350° oven for 7-9 minutes.

Violet's Crescent Cocoons

Makes 10 dozen

2 cups butter or margarine
1 cup powdered sugar
½ teaspoon salt
4 teaspoons vanilla
½ teaspoon butter flavoring
4½ cups flour
1½ cups finely chopped nuts
Additional powdered
    sugar

Cream butter or margarine and sugar. Add salt, vanilla and butter flavoring; mix well. Add flour and nuts and mix thoroughly. Chill 3 hours. Form into crescents. Bake on ungreased cookie sheets at 325° about 20 minutes. Roll in powdered sugar while still warm.

Coffee Tortoni
"a light coffee flavored dessert"

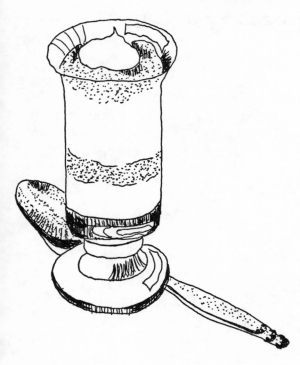

Serves 4

2 egg whites
1 tablespoon instant coffee
⅛ teaspoon salt
2 tablespoons sugar
½ pint whipping cream
¼ cup sugar
1 tablespoon Kahlua or
   creme de cocoa
¼ teaspoon almond extract
½ cup slivered almonds,
   toasted

Combine egg whites, coffee and salt; beat till stiff. Add sugar gradually. Whip cream until it is almost stiff. Continue beating slowly while adding remaining ingredients, except for almonds. Fold whipped cream mixture into the egg whites. Gently fold in the almonds. Spoon into parfait or sherbet glasses and freeze 2 to 3 hours.

Recipes from Iowa with Love...

Each summer we hear the comment that the "corn is knee high by the Fourth of July." Years ago, the farmers may have been pleased with this, but today, with earlier planting and better fertilizers, the corn is often shoulder high by the Fourth of July.

Fourth of July Frozen Fruit Cup

Serves 6

1 6-ounce can frozen
   lemonade
1 6-ounce can frozen
   orange juice
1 10-ounce package frozen
   strawberries
3 or 4 bananas, mashed
1 8-ounce can crushed
   pineapple
¾ cup sugar
2 cups water

Partially thaw frozen juices and strawberries. Mix ingredients together in large bowl. Pour into a 6-8 cup bowl that can go into freezer. Freeze until slushy, stir. Allow 3 hours to freeze before serving.

Recipes from Iowa with Love...

There had to be a better way to fill a fountain pen than with a medicine dropper. W. A. Sheaffer of Fort Madison was determined to find that way, and spent five years developing a pen with a self-filling lever. The Sheaffer Pen Company became a world leader in the manufacture of pens and one of the most important industries in Iowa.

The Next Best Thing to Robert Redford

"a layered dessert of luscious flavors"

Serves 10

½ cup butter or margarine, melted
1 cup sifted flour
1 cup chopped pecans (reserve some for top)
1 8-ounce package cream cheese, softened
1 cup sugar
¼ teaspoon maple flavoring
1 8-ounce carton frozen whipped topping, thawed
1 large package instant chocolate pudding
1 large package instant vanilla pudding
¼ teaspoon almond extract
3 cups cold milk
2 tablespoons grated unsweetened baking chocolate

Mix butter, flour and nuts and press into an oiled 9x13" pan. Bake at 350° for 20 minutes or until lightly browned. Cool thoroughly. Mix cream cheese, sugar and maple flavoring until smooth. Fold in half the whipped topping and spread over cooled crust. Using an electric mixer, beat the puddings, almond extract and milk until smooth and thick. Spread over cream cheese layer. Top with remaining whipped topping, grated chocolate and nuts.

The wild rose is the state flower of Iowa. It is lovely along the roads and fences during the summer months.

Lois' Banana Caramel Chiffon

"creamy and delicious"

Serves 6

1 envelope gelatin
6 tablespoons brown sugar
2 egg yolks
1 cup milk
1 cup mashed banana
1 teaspoon vanilla
2 egg whites
   Whipped cream

Mix gelatin, brown sugar, egg yolks and milk in a saucepan. Cook over low heat, stirring constantly, until mixture comes to a boil. Remove from heat and stir in banana and vanilla. Chill until it is thick enough to form a mound when dropped from a spoon. Beat egg whites until stiff. Fold into the banana mixture and spoon into parfait or sherbet glasses. Chill for 2 hours. Top with whipped cream when ready to serve.

Devonshire Green Grapes

"the perfect touch when you want a light dessert"

Serves 4

3 cups seedless green
    grapes
½ cup sour cream
2 tablespoons brown sugar
  Mint sprigs
  Creme de cacao
    (optional)

Wash grapes and dry thoroughly. Mix sour cream and grapes until grapes are well-coated. Chill several hours. Put into sherbet glasses, sprinkle tops with brown sugar and garnish with a sprig of mint. Pass creme de cacao to spoon over top, if desired.

Mint Dazzler

Serves 18

2 cups vanilla wafer
    crumbs
¼ cup melted butter
1½ cups sifted powdered
    sugar
½ cup butter
3 eggs, slightly beaten
3 1-ounce squares un-
    sweetened chocolate,
    melted
1½ cups whipping cream
1 small package miniature
    marshmallows
½ cup crushed peppermint
    stick candy

Mix wafer crumbs and melted butter; press into a buttered 9×13" cake pan. Cream sugar and butter together. Add eggs and melted chocolate. Beat with electric mixer until light and fluffy. Spread over the crumbs. Set in freezer. Whip cream until stiff; fold in marshmallows. Spread over the chocolate mixture. Sprinkle peppermint stick candy over the top. Freeze 2-3 hours. Remove from freezer 20 minutes before serving.

Ice cream socials are a summer tradition in Iowa. The ice cream is usually homemade from fresh farm cream and eggs. The women serve their special cakes and favorite ice cream toppings, the men discuss weather and farm prices, and the children play softball. Then, everyone sits in the shade and eats as much ice cream as they possibly can.

Homemade Chocolate Sauce

"wonderful topping — and easy to do"

2 cups sugar
1 large can evaporated milk
4 squares unsweetened chocolate
½ cup butter
1 teaspoon vanilla
½ teaspoon salt

Boil sugar and evaporated milk in heavy saucepan for two minutes. Melt chocolate squares in double boiler and add to milk and sugar. Beat till smooth and add butter. Mix well; add vanilla and salt and stir.

Old Fashioned Fudge

"if you've forgotten how good fudge used to taste"

2 cups sugar
⅓ cup cocoa
½ cup milk
¼ cup margarine
½ teaspoon vanilla

Put all ingredients except vanilla into a heavy saucepan and mix. Boil till a drop forms soft ball in cold water. Remove from heat, add vanilla and set in pan of cold water till cool. Beat until stiff and pour onto a buttered plate.

Recipes from Iowa with Love...

Each year thousands of people make a pilgrimage to the Little Brown Church, near Nashua. The hymn, *The Little Brown Church in the Vale*, was written by Dr. William Pitts, and was played and sung for the first time in public at the dedication of the small church. Several hundred couples travel to Nashua each year to be married in the church.

Peanut-Coconut Crunch

Makes 40-50 pieces

4 cups corn flakes
1 cup coconut
1 cup salted peanuts
1 cup sugar
1 cup light corn syrup
½ cup cream

Place corn flakes, coconut and peanuts in a buttered mixing bowl. Combine sugar, syrup and cream in a small saucepan and place over medium heat. Stir until sugar is dissolved. Continue to cook until mixture reaches soft ball stage (238° on a candy thermometer). Pour syrup mixture over the ingredients in the mixing bowl, and stir. Pour into a 9×13″ buttered pan and cut while still warm.

George Washington Carver, born in slavery, became a student at Simpson College in Indianola in 1890. In 1891, he became the first Negro student at Iowa State. His discoveries as an agriculture research chemist and botanist were monumental, and he is particularly remembered for finding 300 uses for the peanut and its shell.

Best Peanut Brittle

Makes 1 pound

1 cup white sugar
1 cup light corn syrup
2 cups raw peanuts
1 tablespoon soda
⅛ teaspoon salt

Mix sugar, syrup and peanuts in a heavy, deep saucepan. Stir until sugar dissolves. Cook until mixture reaches 298° on a candy thermometer. Add soda and salt and pour on a buttered cookie sheet. When cool, break into pieces.

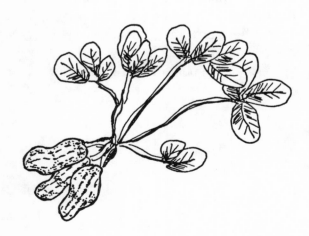

Mimi's Best Toffee Crunch

"a treasured tradition at Christmas"

Makes 1 pound

1 **cup butter**
1 **cup sugar**
2 **tablespoons water**
½ **cup sliced almonds or chopped pecans**
6 **thin milk chocolate bars**

Melt butter in heavy, medium saucepan. Add sugar and stir until dissolved. Add water and cook, stirring often until mixture reaches 290°. Pour into a 9×13" pan that has been buttered and sprinkled with ¼ cup nuts. Lay chocolate bars on top of hot candy; spread when chocolate is melted. Sprinkle remaining nuts over chocolate. When cool, break into pieces.

Super Snack
"good combination"

Makes 1 quart

1 12-ounce package
   chocolate chips
1 15-ounce package raisins
1 12-ounce jar dry roasted
   peanuts

Mix ingredients, and enjoy!

Candy Coated Peanuts

Makes 2 cups

1 cup sugar
½ cup water
2 cups raw peanuts

Mix sugar, water and peanuts together in a skillet or an electric fry pan. Cook 30 minutes or until nuts absorb sugar-water mixture. Turn out on a cookie sheet and bake in a 325° oven for about 50 minutes.

Cream Caramels

"perfect for Christmas giving"

Makes 64 pieces

2 cups sugar
2 cups warm cream
1 cup light corn syrup
½ teaspoon salt
⅓ cup butter
1 teaspoon vanilla
½ cup nuts, chopped

Mix sugar, half the cream, syrup and salt in heavy 3-quart pan. Cook over medium heat for 10 minutes, stirring constantly. Add remaining cream so slowly the mixture does not stop boiling. Cook another 5 minutes. Add butter 1 teaspoon at a time. Turn heat to low and cook to 246°-248° on the candy thermometer. Remove from heat, add vanilla and nuts. Let stand 10 minutes, then stir only enough to mix in the nuts. Pour into a corner of a buttered 8×8″ pan and allow to flow to own level. Do not scrape pan. Cool thoroughly, turn onto cutting board and cut into 1″ squares. Wrap in wax paper.

Recipes from Iowa with Love...

At the turn of the century, a barber in the town of Madrid was determined to make a shampoo better than what was then available. After much testing, he mixed his preparation in a wash boiler, bottled it, and was on his way to becoming "the Shampoo King." His name was F. W. Fitch, and there are still millions of people who can sing the tune that introduced the Fitch Bandwagon radio program.

Paddington's Peanut Logs

"a favorite for children of all ages"

Makes 72

1   cup butter, melted
2   cups graham cracker
     crumbs, finely crushed
1¼ cups creamy peanut
     butter
2   cups powdered sugar
1   12-ounce package
     chocolate chips

Blend all ingredients except chocolate chips thoroughly. Mixture will be very stiff. Roll and shape into 1½" flat-sided logs. Refrigerate for 1 hour. Melt chocolate chips in a double boiler, stirring with a rubber spatula. Using tongs, dip and roll logs in chocolate until completely covered. Place coated logs on wax paper-covered cookie sheet. Chill.

Caramel Popcorn

Makes 8 quarts

2 cups brown sugar
1 cup margarine
½ cup light corn syrup
1 teaspoon salt
   Pinch, cream of tarter
1 teaspoon soda
7½ quarts popped corn

Cook all ingredients, except soda and popcorn, for 5 minutes. Remove from stove and add soda. Add to popcorn and mix well. Spread on 2 large cookie sheets and place in oven at 200° for 1 hour. Stir every 15 minutes. Store in covered containers after cooling.

House
Specialties

Marinade for Pork
"especially good with the Iowa chop"

3 **pounds pork, roast
    or chops**
1 **teaspoon salt**
⅛ **teaspoon pepper**
3 **tablespoons lemon juice**
3 **tablespoons olive oil**
3 **parsley sprigs**
¼ **teaspoon thyme or sage**
1 **bay leaf, crumbled**
1 **clove garlic, mashed**

Rub meat with salt and pepper. Mix the other ingredients in a bowl. Add the pork to the mixture and baste it. Cover bowl with lid or plastic wrap. Marinate for 8 hours, turning and basting meat occasionally during marinating period.

Marinade for Country Ham
"very simple and very special"

1 **ham, any size**
1 **cup orange juice**
1 **cup brown sugar**
1 **cup bourbon**
1 **tablespoon ground cloves**

Place ham in a heavy duty plastic bag. Mix remaining ingredients together and pour over ham in bag. Turn bag occasionally. Allow at least 24 hours for marinating.

Granny's Relish

Makes 28 6-ounce jars

11 cups ground green
    tomatoes
4 cups ground green
    peppers
2 cups ground onions
4 tablespoons salt
3 cups vinegar
6 cups sugar
1 tablespoon dry mustard
1 tablespoon celery seed

Mix tomatoes, peppers, onions and salt together and let stand 1 hour. Drain, and transfer to a large kettle. Add vinegar, sugar, mustard and celery seed. Bring to a boil, lower heat and simmer, uncovered for 20 minutes. Seal in sterile jars.

Zucchini Relish a la Brown

"possibly the best relish to be found"

Makes 7½ pints

6 large zucchini squash, washed
4 large onions
1 red pepper, seeded
1 green pepper, seeded
½ cup salt
3 cups plus 1 tablespoon sugar
2 cups vinegar
½ cup water
2 teaspoons celery seed
1½ teaspoons tumeric

Seed zucchini by slicing lengthwise and running tip of spoon down center portion. Put vegetables through medium grind of food chopper. Put in large bowl, pour salt over the top, and cover with ice water for 1 hour. Drain, rinse with cold water and squeeze out moisture. Set aside. Combine sugar, vinegar, water, celery seed and tumeric in large kettle. Bring to a boil and simmer for 3 minutes. Add vegetables and cook 15 minutes or until mixture become clear. Seal in hot, sterilized jars.

Dieter's Vegetable Pickles
"low-caloried munchies to cure those hunger pangs"

1 cup celery
2 cups carrots
2 cups cauliflower
1 cup green pepper
1 cup zucchini
1 cup green beans
1 cup broccoli stems
1 cup cucumber
Artificial sweetener
   to equal 12 teaspoons
   sugar
¾ cup wine vinegar
¼ cup cider vinegar
¼ cup lemon juice
2 teaspoons salt
1 teaspoon sweet basil
2 4-ounce cans
   mushrooms

Vegetables used (10 cups) can vary according to preference. Cut into bite-size chunks and put into large kettle. Add artificial sweetener, vinegars, lemon juice, salt, basil and mushrooms with their liquid. Bring to a boil; simmer uncovered 5 minutes. Cool and chill. May be used as a salad or as a low-calorie snack. This keeps in the refrigerator up to 4 weeks.

Recipes from Iowa with Love...

Honey was highly prized during the pioneer days when sugar was rare and costly. A strip of land in southeast Iowa that was rich in bee trees containing wild honey was the cause of a quarrel between Missouri and Iowa that became known as the "Honey War." In 1839, Missouri's governor called out troops to claim this strip for his state, and more than a thousand Iowans showed up with pitchforks and a few guns to repel the invaders. No shots were fired, but three honey trees were chopped down.

Honey Apricot Spread

Makes 2 cups

2¼ cups dried apricots
1¼ cups honey
1 teaspoon grated lemon peel
1 teaspoon grated orange peel
½ cup crushed pineapple, drained

Cook apricots in enough water to cover for 5 minutes. Drain and cool slightly. With machine running, add to blender a few at a time, mixing well. Add honey slowly until mixture is thick and creamy. Add lemon, orange peel and pineapple. Refrigerate until ready to serve. Can be kept in the refrigerator up to 2 weeks.

Summer Hummer

"a combination dessert and after-dinner drink"

Serves 6

6 ounces coffee liqueur
6 ounces rum
2½ cups vanilla ice cream

Beat all ingredients together until blended. Serve in champagne-sherbet glasses.

Yellow Birds

"perfect for a summer afternoon with friends"

Serves 8

1 6-ounce can frozen orange juice
12 ounces canned pineapple juice
12 ounces white rum
6 ounces creme de banana
18 ounces water

Mix together in a large glass pitcher. Add a generous amount of ice and serve in your most summery glasses.

Ila's Rum Slush

Serves 1

½ cup crushed ice
2 ounces light rum
1 ounce lemon juice
2 tablespoons powdered sugar
1 egg white
1 thin lemon slice

Place all ingredients except lemon slice in a blender. Blend on high speed 1 minute. Pour into chilled cocktail glass without straining. Use lemon slice for garnish.

Index

A

B

Contributors

Our thanks to the following great Iowa cooks who have shared their favorite recipes with us. We regret that we were unable to include many recipes because of lack of space.

Anderson, Helen	Des Moines	Klein, Mrs. Kenton	Des Moines
Anderson, Jean Ann	New Hampton	Koch, Betty	Des Moines
Arterburn, Dale	Des Moines	Kufner, Leslie	Fairfield
Bailey, Beverly	Nashua	Lamport, Jan	Indianola
Bottorff, Ron	Des Moines	Larson, Mrs. Robert	Des Moines
Bradley, Barbara	Des Moines	Levine, Caroline	Des Moines
Brenton, Babette	Des Moines	Lock, Joyce	Des Moines
Brodie, Beverly	Akron	Linn, Barbara	Des Moines
Brower, Steve and Kathy	Burlington	Maher, Mrs. Louis	Des Moines
Brown, Helen	Des Moines	Martin, Clara	Charles City
Brown, Mary Kay	Des Moines	Miller, Darlene	Clear Lake
Burns, Mrs. Frank	Des Moines	Montross, Patricia	Winterset
Callison, Mrs. James	Des Moines	Orr, Marcie Taggart	Indianola
Carter, Pam	Burlington	Parker, Janet	Des Moines
Cartwright, Emily F.	Marshalltown	Rambo, Carol	Decorah
Clark, Lois	Burlington	Ray, Mrs. Robert	Cedar Rapids
Cram, Mrs. Carroll	Des Moines	Reichardt, Sue	Des Moines
Crispin, Mrs. William	Des Moines	Robison, Pat	Davenport
DeVries, Dottie	Pella	Roemig, Betty J.	Homestead
Doherty, Jerry	Fort Madison	Royer, Betty	Jefferson
Downing, Ardene	Indianola	Sandvold, Lois	Nevada
Erbe, Ednamay	Boone	Schlenker, Charlotte	Indianola
Evans, Jane E.	Des Moines	Schukei, Mr. and Mrs. Bob	Clear Lake
Fangman, Al	Clear Lake	Sheaffer, Mrs. John D.	Fort Madison
Frank, Helen J.	Centerville	Shiffler, Dr. and Mrs. Kirby	Des Moines
Freeman, Mrs. Claude	Des Moines	Siberell, Mrs. Stan	Des Moines
Frick, Flora	Williamsburg	Sidney, Mrs. Ross	Des Moines
Grundler, Pam	Grinnell	Slick, Jewel	Des Moines
Hagen, Lillian	Homestead	Sloan, Mrs. Chet	Des Moines
Hanson, Mrs. John K.	Forest City	Smith, Barbara	Grundy Center
Harmon, Muffie	Des Moines	Speicher, Janet	Waukee
Harris, John R.	Des Moines	Springer, Babs	West Des Moines
Hauth, Betty	New Hampton	Stegman, John	Britt
Heggen, Mrs. Roy	Des Moines	Strawtown Inn	Pella
Hein, Mrs. Douglas	Des Moines	Tillotson, Karla	Des Moines
Hein, Mrs. Herb	Des Moines	Tucker, Thelma	Storm Lake
Hilburn, Ruby	Des Moines	Utterback, Betty	Grinnell
Hirsch, Esther	Burlington	Warner, Ana Maria	Burlington
Hufford, Violet	Muscatine	Wellborn, Deena	Grinnell
Hunter, Dan	Des Moines	Wilson, Mr. and Mrs. George	West Des Moines
Iowa Machine Shed	Davenport	Wine, Mary	Des Moines
Iowa Pork Producers	Des Moines	Wittmack, Dee	Des Moines
Juhl, Colleen	Council Bluffs	Wood, Pauline	Ellston
Kahn, Bobbie	Clear Lake	Woodin, Marilyn	Kalona
Kavanagh, Judith	Ames	Yeglin, Dorothy	Des Moines
Kelley, Iris	Scranton	Young, Marlys	Ames
Kiess, Eileen	Des Moines	Young, Mildred	Des Moines

OUR SPECIAL THANKS TO:

Dan Hunter for use of his song, "Walking Beans"
George Mills for advice on historical facts about Iowa
Marcie Taggert Orr for help in the collecting of recipes
William Wagner for use of his sketch of Terrace Hill.

The following Iowa cookbooks for allowing a reprint of one of their recipes:

Better Homes and Gardens, Meredith Corporation,
    Des Moines,
Country Cooking, Beverly Brodie, Akron
The Mousse and Me, recipes of JoAnn Fangman, Clear Lake
Pella Collector's Cookbook, Women's Auxilliary of Central
    College, Pella
A Pictorial History of Food in Iowa, Living History Farms,
    Des Moines
A Taste of Terrace Hill, Terrace Hill Society, Des Moines
Old Threshers Cookbook, Mt. Pleasant

THE FOLLOWING SOURCES WERE HELPFUL IN WRIT-
ING THE PARAGRAPHS ABOUT IOWA:

Discovering Historic Iowa, LeRoy G. Pratt
From Cabin to Capital, LeRoy G. Pratt
General Dodge House, Council Bluffs
Hawkeye Lore, Bernice Reida and Ann Irwin
Herbert Hoover Presidential Library, West Branch
Iowa, a History, Joseph Frazier Wall
Iowan Magazine, Des Moines
Iowa's Amazing Past, George Mills
Iowa, 1982 Statistical Profile, Iowa Development Commission
Living History Farms, Des Moines
Portrait of Iowa, John M. Zielinski
They Came to Iowa, H. L. Moeller

Additional copies of *"Recipes From Iowa With Love,"* can be ordered for $8.50, plus $1.00 for postage and handling. from:

New Boundary Designs, Inc.
1453 Park Road
Chanhassen, MN 55317

Other cookbooks available through New Boundary Designs:

Make checks payable to:
New Boundary Designs, Inc.
Add $1.00 for postage and handling